Helene Hanff has been writing letters all her life, but in addition she has studied playwriting at the Theatre Guild, written for 'The Hallmark Hall of Fame' and for 'Ellery Queen'. She has written many books for children as well as articles for the *New Yorker* and *Harper*'s magazines. In this volume we have included two of her books: *The Duchess of Bloomsbury Street* and *84 Charing Cross Road*.

D0234351

F. P. D. In Memoriam

Helene Hanff

84 Charing Cross Road

Futura
Macdonald & Co
London & Sydney

A Futura Book

First published in this form in 1976
by Futura Publications Limited

The Duchess of Bloomsbury Street
first published in Great Britain in 1974
by André Deutsch Ltd

84 Charing Cross Road
first published in Great Britain in 1971
by André Deutsch Ltd
Reprinted this edition 1981, 1982

Copyright © 1970 and 1973 by Helene Hanff

This book is sold subject to the condition
that it shall not, by way of trade or
otherwise, be lent, re-sold, hired out or
otherwise circulated without the publisher's
prior consent in any form of binding or
cover other than that in which it is
published and without a similar condition
including this condition being imposed on the
subsequent purchaser

ISBN 0 8600 7438 2

Printed in Great Britain by
Hazell Watson & Viney Ltd
Aylesbury, Bucks

Futura Publications
A Division of
Macdonald & Co (Publishers) Ltd
Maxwell House
Worship Street
London EC2A 2EN

14 East 95th St.
New York City

OCTOBER 5, 1949

Marks & Co.
84, Charing Cross Road
London, W.C. 2
England

Gentlemen :

Your ad in the *Saturday Review of Literature* says that you specialize in out-of-print books. The phrase 'antiquarian book-sellers' scares me somewhat, as I equate 'antique' with expensive. I am a poor writer with an antiquarian taste in books and all the things I want are impossible to get over here except in very expensive rare editions, or in Barnes & Noble's grimy, marked-up schoolboy copies.

I enclose a list of my most pressing problems. If you have clean secondhand copies of any of the books on the list, for no more than $5.00 each, will you consider this a purchase order and send them to me?

Very truly yours,

Helene Hanff
(Miss) Helene Hanff

25TH OCTOBER, 1949

Miss Helene Hanff
14 East 95th Street
New York 28, New York
U.S.A.

Dear Madam,

In reply to your letter of October 5th, we have managed to clear up two thirds of your problem. The three Hazlitt essays you want are contained in the Nonesuch Press edition of his *Selected Essays* and the Stevenson is found in *Virginibus Puerisque*. We are sending nice copies of both these by Book Post and we trust they will arrive safely in due course and that you will be pleased with them. Our invoice is enclosed with the books.

The Leigh Hunt essays are not going to be so easy but we will see if we can find an attractive volume with them all in. We haven't the Latin Bible you describe but we have a Latin New Testament, also a Greek New Testament, ordinary modern editions in cloth binding. Would you like these?

Yours faithfully,

FPD
For MARKS & CO.

14 East 95th St.
New York City

NOVEMBER 3, 1949

Marks & Co.
84, Charing Cross Road
London, W.C. 2
England

Gentlemen :

The books arrived safely, the Stevenson is so fine it embarrasses my orange-crate bookshelves, I'm almost afraid to handle such soft vellum and heavy cream-colored pages. Being used to the dead-white paper and stiff cardboardy covers of American books, I never knew a book could be such a joy to the touch.

A Britisher whose girl lives upstairs translated the £1/17/6 for me and says I owe you $5.30 for the two books. I hope he got it right. I enclose a $5 bill and a single, please use the 70¢ toward the price of the New Testaments, both of which I want.

Will you please translate your prices hereafter? I don't add too well in plain American, I haven't a prayer of ever mastering bilingual arithmetic.

Yours,

Helene Hanff

I hope 'madam' doesn't mean over there what it does here.

MARKS & CO., Booksellers
84, Charing Cross Road
London, W.C. 2

9TH NOVEMBER, 1949

Miss Helene Hanff
14 East 95th Street
New York 28, New York
U.S.A.

Dear Miss Hanff,

Your six dollars arrived safely, but we should feel very much easier if you would send your remittances by postal money order in future, as this would be quite a bit safer for you than entrusting dollar bills to the mails.

We are very happy you liked the Stevenson so much. We have sent off the New Testaments, with an invoice listing the amount due in both pounds and dollars, and we hope you will be pleased with them.

Yours faithfully,

FPD
For MARKS & CO.

WHAT KIND OF A BLACK PROTESTANT BIBLE IS THIS?

Kindly inform the Church of England they have loused up the most beautiful prose ever written, whoever told them to tinker with the Vulgate Latin? They'll burn for it, you mark my words.

It's nothing to me, I'm Jewish myself. But I have a Catholic sister-in-law, a Methodist sister-in-law, a whole raft of Presbyterian cousins (through my Great-Uncle Abraham who converted) and an aunt who's a Christian Science healer, and I like to think *none* of them would countenance this Anglican Latin Bible if they knew it existed. (As it happens, they don't know Latin existed.)

Well, the hell with it. I've been using my Latin teacher's Vulgate, what I imagine I'll do is just not give it back till you find me one of my own.

I enclose $4 to cover the $3.88 due you, buy yourself a cup of coffee with the 12c. There's no post office near here and I am not running all the way down to Rockefeller Plaza to stand in line for a $3.88 money order. If I wait till I get down there for something else, I won't have the $3.88 any more. I have implicit faith in the U.S. Airmail and His Majesty's Postal Service.

Have you got a copy of Landor's *Imaginary Conversations*? I think there are several volumes, the one I want is the one with the Greek conversations. If it contains a dialogue between Aesop and Rhodope, that'll be the volume I want.

Helene Hanff

26TH NOVEMBER, 1949

Miss Helene Hanff
14 East 95th Street
New York 28, New York
U.S.A.

Dear Miss Hanff,

Your four dollars arrived safely and we have credited the 12 cents to your account.

We happen to have in stock Volume II of the Works & Life of Walter Savage Landor which contains the Greek dialogues including the one mentioned in your letter, as well as the Roman dialogues. It is an old edition published in 1876, not very handsome but well bound and a good clean copy, and we are sending it off to you today with invoice enclosed.

I am sorry we made the mistake with the Latin Bible and will try to find a Vulgate for you. Not forgetting Leigh Hunt.

Yours faithfully,

FPD
For MARKS & CO.

December 8, 1949

Sir :

(It feels witless to keep writing 'Gentlemen' when the same solitary soul is obviously taking care of everything for me.)

Savage Landor arrived safely and promptly fell open to a Roman dialogue where two cities had just been destroyed by war and everybody was being crucified and begging passing Roman soldiers to run them through and end the agony. It'll be a relief to turn to Aesop and Rhodope where all you have to worry about is a famine. I do love secondhand books that open to the page some previous owner read oftenest. The day Hazlitt came he opened to 'I hate to read new books,' and I hollered 'Comrade !' to whoever owned it before me.

I enclose a dollar which Brian (British boy friend of Kay upstairs) says will cover the /8/ I owe you, you forgot to translate it.

Now then. Brian told me you are all rationed to 2 ounces of meat per family per week and one egg per person per month and I am simply appalled. He has a catalogue from a British firm here which flies food from Denmark to his mother, so I am sending a small Christmas present to Marks & Co. I hope there will be enough to go round, he says the Charing Cross Road bookshops are 'all quite small.'

I'm sending it c/o you, FPD, whoever you are.

Noel.

Helene Hanff

14 East 95th St.

DECEMBER 9, 1949

FPD ! CRISIS !

I sent that package off. The chief item in it was a 6-pound ham, I figured you could take it to a butcher and get it sliced up so everybody would have some to take home.

But I just noticed on your last invoice it says. 'B. Marks. M. Cohen.' Props.

ARE THEY KOSHER? I could rush a tongue over.
ADVISE PLEASE !

Helene Hanff

MARKS & CO., Booksellers
84, Charing Cross Road
London, W.C. 2

20TH DECEMBER, 1949

Miss Helene Hanff
14 East 95th Street
New York 28, New York
U.S.A.

Dear Miss Hanff,

Just a note to let you know that your gift parcel arrived safely today and the contents have been shared out between the staff. Mr. Marks and Mr. Cohen insisted that we divide it up among ourselves and not include 'the bosses.' I should just like to add that everything in the parcel was something that we either never see or can only be had through the black market. It was extremely kind and generous of you to think of us in this way and we are all extremely grateful.

We all wish to express our thanks and send our greetings and best wishes for 1950.

Yours faithfully,

Frank Doel
For MARKS & CO.

Frank Doel, what are you DOING over there, you are not doing ANYthing, you are just sitting AROUND.

Where is Leigh Hunt? Where is the *Oxford Verse*? Where is the Vulgate and dear goofy John Henry, I thought they'd be such nice uplifting reading for Lent and NOTHING do you send me.

you leave me sitting here writing long margin notes in library books that don't belong to me, some day they'll find out i did it and take my library card away.

I have made arrangements with the Easter bunny to bring you an Egg, he will get over there and find you have died of Inertia.

I require a book of love poems with spring coming on. *No Keats or Shelley*, send me poets who can make love without slobbering — Wyatt or Jonson or somebody, use your own judgment. Just a nice book preferably small enough to stick in a slacks pocket and take to Central Park.

Well, don't just sit there! Go find it! i swear i don't know how that shop keeps going.

MARKS & CO., Booksellers
84, Charing Cross Road
London, W.C. 2

7TH APRIL, 1950

Miss Helene Hanff
14 East 95th Street
New York 28, New York
U.S.A.

Dear Miss Hanff,

I have to thank you for the very welcome Easter parcel which arrived safely yesterday. We were all delighted to see the tins and the box of shell eggs, and the rest of the staff joins me in thanking you for your very kind and generous thought of us.

I am sorry we haven't been able to send you any of the books you want. About the book of love poems, now and then we do get such a volume as you describe. We have none in stock at the moment but shall look out for one for you.

Again, many thanks for the parcel.

Faithfully yours,

Frank Doel
For MARKS & CO.

MARKS & CO., Booksellers
84, Charing Cross Road.
London, W.C. 2

Dear Miss Hanff,

Please don't let Frank know I'm writing this but every time I send you a bill I've been dying to slip in a little note and he might not think it quite proper of me. That sounds stuffy and he's not, he's quite nice really, very nice in fact, it's just that he does rather look on you as his private correspondent as all your letters and parcels are addressed to him. But I just thought I would write to you on my own.

We all love your letters and try to imagine what you must be like. I've decided you're young and very sophisticated and smart-looking. Old Mr. Martin thinks you must be quite studious-looking in spite of your wonderful sense of humor. Why don't you send us a snapshot? We should love to have it.

If you're curious about Frank, he's in his late thirties, quite nice-looking, married to a very sweet Irish girl, I believe she's his second wife.

Everyone was so grateful for the parcel. My little ones (girl 5, boy 4) were in Heaven – with the raisins and egg I was actually able to make them a cake !

I do hope you don't mind my writing. Please don't mention it when you write to Frank.

With best wishes,

Cecily Farr

P.S. I shall put my home address on the back of this in case you should ever want anything sent you from London.

C.F.

APRIL 10, 1950

Dear Cecily –

And a *very* bad cess to Old Mr. Martin, tell him I'm so unstudious I never even went to college. I just happen to have peculiar taste in books, thanks to a Cambridge professor named Quiller-Couch, known as Q, whom I fell over in a library when I was 17. And I'm about as smart-looking as a Broadway panhandler. I live in moth-eaten sweaters and wool slacks, they don't give us any heat here in the daytime. It's a 5-story brownstone and all the other tenants go out to work at 9 A.M. and don't come home till 6 – and why should the landlord heat the building for one small script-reader/writer working at home on the ground floor?

Poor Frank, I give him such a hard time, I'm always bawling him out for something. I'm only teasing, but I know he'll take me seriously. I keep trying to puncture that proper British reserve, if he gets ulcers I did it.

Please write and tell me about London, I live for the day when I step off the boat-train and feel its dirty sidewalks under my feet. I want to walk up Berkeley Square and down Wimpole Street and stand in St. Paul's where John Donne preached and sit on the step Elizabeth sat on when she refused to enter the Tower, and like that. A newspaper man I know, who was stationed in London during the war, says tourists go to England with preconceived notions, so they always find exactly what they go looking for. I told him I'd go looking for the England of English literature, and he said :

'Then it's there.'

Regards –

Helene Hanff

20TH SEPTEMBER, 1950

Miss Helene Hanff
14 East 95th Street
New York 28, New York
U.S.A.

Dear Miss Hanff,

It is such a long time since we wrote to you I hope you do not think we have forgotten all about your wants.

Anyway, we now have in stock the *Oxford Book of English Verse*, printed on India paper, original blue cloth binding, 1905, inscription in ink on the flyleaf but a good second-hand copy, price $2.00 We thought we had better quote before sending, in case you have already purchased a copy.

Some time ago you asked us for Newman's *Idea of a University*. Would you be interested in a copy of the first edition? We have just purchased one, particulars as follows :

NEWMAN (JOHN HENRY, D.D.) Discourses on the Scope and Nature of University Education, Addressed to the Catholics of Dublin. First edition, 8vo. calf, Dublin, 1852. A few pages a little age-stained and spotted but a good copy in a sound binding.   Price – $6.00

In case you would like them, we will put both books on one side until you have time to reply.

With kind regards,
Yours faithfully,

Frank Doel
For MARKS & CO.

he has a first edition of Newman's University for six bucks, do i want it, he asks innocently.

Dear Frank :

Yes, I want it. I won't be fit to live with myself. I've never cared about first editions per se, but a first edition of THAT book – !

oh my.

i can just see it.

Send the *Oxford Verse*, too, please. Never wonder if I've found something somewhere else, I don't look anywhere else any more. Why should I run all the way down to 17th St. to buy dirty, badly made books when I can buy clean, beautiful ones from you without leaving the typewriter? From where I sit, London's a lot closer than 17th Street.

Enclosed please God please find $8. Did I tell you about Brian's lawsuit? He buys physics tomes from a technical book-shop in London, he's not sloppy and haphazard like me, he bought an expensive set and went down to Rockefeller Plaza and stood in line and got a money order and cabled it or whatever you do with it, he's a businessman, he does things right.

the money order got lost in transit.

Up His Majesty's Postal Service !

HH

am sending very small parcel to celebrate first edition, Overseas Associates finally sent me my own catalogue.

2ND OCTOBER, 1950

Dear Helene,

I brought the enclosed snapshots to the shop with me weeks ago, but we've been frightfully busy so have had no chance to send them on to you. They were taken in Norfolk where Doug (my husband) is stationed with the RAF. None of them very flattering of me, but they are the best we have of the children and the one of Doug alone is very good.

My dear, I do hope you get your wish to come to England. Why not save your pennies and come next summer? Mummy and Daddy have a house in Middlesex and would be delighted to put you up.

Megan Wells (secretary to the bosses) and I are going on a week's holiday to Jersey (Channel Islands) in July. Why don't you come with us and then you could economize the rest of the month in Middlesex?

Ben Marks is trying to see what I'm writing so shall have to close.

Sincerely,

Cecily

OCTOBER 15, 1950

WELL ! ! !

All I have to say to YOU, Frank Doel, is we live in depraved, destructive and degenerate times when a bookshop – a BOOKSHOP – starts tearing up beautiful old books to use as wrapping paper. I said to John Henry when he stepped out of it :

'Would you believe a thing like that, Your Eminence?' and he said he wouldn't. You tore that book up in the middle of a major battle and I don't even know which war it was.

The Newman arrived almost a week ago and I'm just beginning to recover. I keep it on the table with me all day, every now and then I stop typing and reach over and touch it. Not because it's a first edition; I just never saw a book so beautiful. I feel vaguely guilty about owning it. All that gleaming leather and gold stamping and beautiful type belongs in the pine-panelled library of an English country home; it wants to be read by the fire in a gentleman's leather easy chair – not on a secondhand studio couch in a one-room hovel in a broken-down brownstone front.

I want the Q anthology. I'm not sure how much it was, I lost your last letter. I think it was about two bucks, I'll enclose two singles, if I owe you more let me know.

Why don't you wrap it in pages LCXII and LCXIII so I can at least find out who won the battle and what war it was?

HH

P.S. Have you got Sam Pepy's diary over there? I need him for long winter evenings.

1ST NOVEMBER, 1950

Miss Helene Hanff
14 East 95th Street
New York 28, New York
U.S.A.

Dear Miss Hanff,

I am sorry for the delay in answering your letter but I have been away out of town for a week or so and am now busy trying to catch up on my correspondence.

First of all, please don't worry about us using old books such as Clarendon's Rebellion for wrapping. In this particular case they were just two odd volumes with the covers detached and nobody in their right senses would have given us a shilling for them.

The Quiller-Couch anthology, *The Pilgrim's Way*, has been sent to you by Book Post. The balance due was $1.85 so your $2 more than covered it. We haven't a copy of Pepys' *Diary* in stock at the moment but shall look out for one for you.

With best wishes,
Yours faithfully,

F. Doel
For MARKS & CO.

MARKS & CO., Booksellers
84, Charing Cross Road
London, W.C. 2

2ND FEBRUARY, 1951

Miss Helene Hanff
14 East 95th Street
New York 28, New York
U.S.A.

Dear Miss Hanff,

We are glad you liked the 'Q' anthology. We have no copy of the *Oxford Book of English Prose* in stock at the moment but will try to find one for you.

About the *Sir Roger de Coverley Papers*, we happen to have in stock a volume of eighteenth century essays which includes a good selection of them as well as essays by Chesterfield and Goldsmith. It is edited by Austin Dobson and is quite a nice edition and as it is only $1.15 we have sent it off to you by Book Post. If you want a more complete collection of Addison & Steele let me know and I will try to find one.

There are six of us in the shop, not including Mr. Marks and Mr. Cohen.

Faithfully yours,

Frank Doel
For MARKS & CO.

20-2-51

Helene my dear –

There are many ways of doing it but Mummy and I think this is the simplest for you to try. Put a cup of flour, an egg, a half cup of milk and a good shake of salt into a large bowl and beat altogether until it is the consistency of thick cream. Put in the frig for several hours. 'It's best if you make it in the morning.) When you put your roast in the oven, put in an extra pan to heat. Half an hour before your roast is done, pour a bit of the roast grease into the baking pan, just enough to cover the bottom will do. The pan must be *very hot*. Now pour the pudding in and the roast and pudding will be ready at the same time.

I don't know quite how to describe it to someone who has never seen it, but a good Yorkshire Pudding will puff up very high and brown and crisp and when you cut into it you will find that it is hollow inside.

The RAF is still keeping Doug in Norfolk and we are firmly hoarding your Christmas tins until he comes home, but my dear, what a celebration we shall have with them when he does! I do think you oughtn't to spend your money like that!

Must fly and post this if you're to have it for Brian's birthday dinner, do let me know if it's a success.

Love,

Cecily

FEBRUARY 25, 1951

Dear Cecily –

Yorkshire Pudding out of this world, we have nothing like it, I had to describe it to somebody as a high, curved, smooth, empty waffle.

Please don't worry about what the food parcels cost, I don't know whether Overseas Asso. is non-profit or duty-free or what, but they are monstrous cheap, that whole Christmas parcel cost less than my turkey. They do have a few rich parcels with things like standing rib-roasts and legs of lamb, but even those are so cheap compared with what they cost in the butcher shops that it kills me not to be able to send them. I have such a time with the catalogue, I spread it out on the rug and debate the relative merits of Parcel 105 (includes-one-dozen-eggs-and-a-tin-of-sweet-biscuits) and Parcel 217B (two-dozen-eggs-and-NO-sweet-biscuits), I hate the one-dozen egg parcels, what is two eggs for anybody to take home? But Brian says the powdered ones taste like glue. So it's a problem.

A producer who likes my plays (but not enough to produce them) just phoned. He's producing a TV series, do I want to write for television? 'Two bills,' he said carelessly, which it turned out means $200. And me a $40-a-week script-reader! I go down to see him tomorrow, keep your fingers crossed.

Best –

helene

MARKS & CO., Booksellers
84, Charing Cross Road
London, W.C. 2

4TH APRIL, 1951

Helene dear —

Your marvelous Easter parcels arrived safely and everyone is quite upset because Frank left the city on business for the firm the next morning and so hasn't written to thank you, and of course no one else quite dares to write to Frank's Miss Hanff.

My dear, the *meat!* I really don't think you should spend your money like that. It must have cost a packet! Bless you for your kind heart.

Here comes Ben Marks with work so must close.

Love,

Cecily

Earl's Terrace
Kensington High St.
London, W. 8

5TH APRIL, 1951

Dear Miss Hanff,

This is just to let you know that your Easter parcels to Marks & Co. arrived safely a few days ago but have not been acknowledged as Frank Doel is away from the office on business for the firm.

We were all quite dazzled to see the meat. And the eggs and tins were so very welcome. I did feel I must write and tell you how exceedingly grateful we all are for your kindness and generosity.

We all hope that you will be able to come to England one of these days. We should do our best to make your trip a happy one.

Sincerely,

Megan Wells

5TH APRIL, 1951

Dear Miss Hanff :

For nearly two years I have been working as a cataloguer at Marks & Co, and would like to thank you very much for my share-out in the parcels which you've been sending.

I live with my great-aunt who is 75, and I think that if you had seen the look of delight on her face when I brought home the meat and the tin of tongue, you would have realized just how grateful we are. It's certainly good to know that someone so many miles away can be so kind and generous to people they haven't even seen, and I think that everyone in the firm feels the same.

If at any time you know of anything that you would like sent over from London, I will be most happy to see to it for you.

Sincerely,

Bill Humphries

MARKS & CO., Booksellers
84, Charing Cross Road
London, W.C. 2

Miss Helene Hanff
14 East 95th Street
New York 28, New York
U.S.A.

Dear Miss Hanff,

I expect you are getting a bit worried that we have not written to thank you for your parcels and are probably thinking that we are an ungrateful lot. The truth is that I have been chasing round the country in and out of various stately homes of England trying to buy a few books to fill up our sadly depleted stock. My wife was starting to call me the lodger who just went home for bed and breakfast, but of course when I arrived home with a nice piece of MEAT, to say nothing of dried eggs and ham, then she thought I was a fine fellow and all was forgiven. It is a long time since we saw so much meat all in one piece.

We should like to express our appreciation in some way or other, so we are sending by Book Post today a little book which I hope you will like. I remember you asked me for a volume of Elizabethan love poems some time ago – well, this the nearest I can get to it.

Yours faithfully,

Frank Doel
For MARKS & CO.

To Helene Hanff, with best
wishes and grateful thanks for
many kindnesses, from all
at 84, Charing Cross Road, London.
April, 1951

APRIL 16, 1951

To All at 84, Charing Cross Road :

Thank you for the beautiful book. I've never owned a book before with pages edged all round in gold. Would you believe it arrived on my birthday?

I wish you hadn't been so over-courteous about putting the inscription on a card instead of on the flyleaf. It's the bookseller coming out in you all, you were afraid you'd decrease its value. You would have increased it for the present owner. (And possibly for the future owner. I love inscriptions on flyleaves and notes in margins, I like the comradely sense of turning pages someone else turned, and reading passages some one long gone has called my attention to.)

And why didn't you sign your names? I expect Frank wouldn't let you, he probably doesn't want me writing love letters to anybody but him.

I send you greetings from America – faithless friend that she is, pouring millions into rebuilding Japan and Germany while letting England starve. Some day, God willing, I'll get over there and apologize personally for my country's sins (and by the time i come home my country will certainly have to apologize for mine).

Thank you again for the beautiful book, I shall try very hard not to get gin and ashes all over it, it's really much too fine for the likes of me.

Yours,

Helene Hanff

SEPTEMBER 10, 1951

Dearheart –

It is the loveliest old shop straight out of Dickens, you
would go absolutely out of your mind over it.

There are stalls outside and I stopped and leafed through
a few things just to establish myself as a browser before
wandering in. It's dim inside, you smell the shop before you
see it, it's a lovely smell, I can't articulate it easily, but it
combines must and dust and age, and walls of wood and
floors of wood. Toward the back of the shop at the left there's
a desk with a work-lamp on it, a man was sitting there, he
was about fifty with a Hogarth nose, he looked up and said
'Good afternoon?' in a North Country accent and I said I
just wanted to browse and he said please do.

The shelves go on forever. They go up to the ceiling and
they're very old and kind of grey, like old oak that has ab-
sorbed so much dust over the years they no longer are their
true color. There's a print section, or rather a long print
table, with Cruikshank and Rackham and Spy and all those
old wonderful English caricaturists and illustrators that I'm
not smart enough to know a lot about, and there are some
lovely old, old illustrated magazines.

I stayed for about half an hour hoping your Frank or one
of the girls would turn up, but it was one-ish when I went in,
I gather they were all out to lunch and I couldn't stay any
longer.

As you see, the notices were not sensational but we're told
they're good enough to assure us a few months' run, so I
went apartment-hunting yesterday and found a nice little
'bed-sitter' in Knightsbridge, I don't have the address here,
I'll send it or you can call my mother.

We have no food problems, we eat in restaurants and hotels, the best places like Claridge's get all the roast beef and chops they want. The prices are astronomical but the exchange rate is so good we can afford it. Of course if I were the English I would loathe us, instead of which they are absolutely wonderful to us, we're invited to everybody's home and everybody's club.

The only thing we can't get is sugar or sweets in any form, for which I personally thank God, I intend to lose ten pounds over here.

Write me.

Love,

Maxine

Maxine, bless your golden heart, what a peachy description, you write better than I do.

I called your mother for your address, she said to tell you the sugar cubes and Nestle bars are on the way, I thought you were dieting?

I don't like to sound bitter, but I would like to know what YOU ever did that the good Lord lets YOU browse around my bookshop while I'm stuck on 95th St. writing the TV 'Adventures of Ellery Queen.' Did I tell you we're not allowed to use a lipstick-stained cigarette for a clue? We're sponsored by the Bayuk Cigar Co. and we're not allowed to mention the word 'cigarette.' We can have ashtrays on the set but they can't have any cigarette butts in them. They can't have cigar butts either, they're not pretty. All an ashtray can have in it is a wrapped, unsmoked Bayuk cigar.

And you hobnobbing with Gielgud at Claridge's.

Write me about London – the tube, the Inns of Court, Mayfair, the corner where the Globe Theatre stood, anything, I'm not fussy. Write me about Knightbridge, it sounds green and gracious in Eric Coates' London Suite. Or London Again Suite.

xxxx

hh

WHAT KIND OF A PEPYS' DIARY DO YOU CALL THIS?

this is not pepys' diary, this is some busybody editor's miserable collection of EXCERPTS from pepys' diary may he rot.

i could just spit.

where is jan. 12, 1668, where his wife chased him out of bed and round the bedroom with a red-hot poker?

where is sir w. pen's son that was giving everybody so much trouble with his Quaker notions? ONE mention does he get in this whole pseudo-book. and me from philadelphia.

i enclose two limp singles, i will make do with this thing till you find me a real Pepys. THEN i will rip up this ersatz book, page by page, AND WRAP THINGS IN IT.

HH

P.S. Fresh eggs or powdered for Xmas? I know the powdered last longer but 'fresh farm eggs flown from Denmark' have got to taste better, you want to take a vote on it?

MARKS & CO., Booksellers
84, Charing Cross Road
London, W.C. 2

20TH OCTOBER, 1951

Miss Helene Hanff
14 East 95th Street
New York 28, New York
U.S.A.

Dear Miss Hanff,

First of all, let me apologize for the Pepys. I was honestly under the impression that it was the complete Braybrooke edition and I can understand how you must have felt when you found your favorite passages missing. I promise to look at the next reasonably priced copy that comes along, and if it contains the passage you mention in your letter I will send it along.

I am glad to say I have managed to dig out a few books for you from a private library that we have just bought. There is a Leigh Hunt which includes most of the essays you like, also a Vulgate New Testament which I hope will be O.K. I have also included a Dictionary to the Vulgate which you might find useful. There is also a volume of 20th century English essays, though it contains only one by Hilaire Belloc and nothing to do with bathrooms. Enclosed is our invoice for 17s 6d. or approximately $2.50, all that is due us on the books as you had a credit balance with us of nearly $2.00.

About the eggs – I have talked to the rest of the inmates here and we all seem to think that the fresh ones would be nicer. As you say, they would not last so long but they would taste so much better.

We are all hoping for better times after the Election. If Churchill and Company get in, as I think and hope they will, it will cheer everyone up immensely.

With best wishes,
Yours sincerely,

Frank Doel
For MARKS & CO.

November 2, 1951

Dear Speed –

You dizzy me, rushing Leigh Hunt and the Vulgate over here whizbang like that. You probably don't realize it, but it's hardly more than two years since I ordered them. You keep going at this rate you're gonna give yourself a heart attack.

that's mean. You go to so much trouble for me and i never even thank you, i just needle you, it's mean. I really am grateful for all the pains you take for me. I enclose three dollars, I'm sorry about the top one, I spilled coffee on it and it wouldn't sponge off but I think it's still good, you can still read it.

Do you carry hard-cover vocal scores, by any chance? Like Bach's St. Matthew Passion and Handel's Messiah? I could probably get them here at Schirmer's, but they're 50 cold blocks from where I live so I thought I'd ask you first.

Congratulations on Churchill & Co., hope he loosens up your rations a little.

Is your name Welsh?

HH

MARKS & CO., Booksellers
84, Charing Cross Road
London, W.C. 2

Miss Helene Hanff
14 East 95th Street
New York 28, New York

Dear Miss Hanff,

You will be glad to know that the two boxes of eggs and the tins of tongue have all arrived safely and once again we all wish to thank you most sincerely for your extreme generosity. Mr. Martin, one of the older members of our staff, has been on the sick list for some time and we therefore let him have the lion's share of the eggs, one whole boxful in fact, and of course he was delighted to get them. The tins of tongue look very inviting and will be a welcome addition to our larders, and in my case will be put on one side for a special occasion.

I enquired at all the local music shops but was unable to get the *Messiah* or Bach's *St. Matthew Passion* in stiff covers in clean, secondhand copies, and then I found they were available from the publisher in new editions. Their prices seemed a bit high, but I thought I had better get them and they have been sent by Book Post a few days ago, so should arrive any day now. Our invoice, total £1/10/ = ($4.20) is enclosed with the books.

We are sending you a little gift for Christmas. It is linen and we do hope you will not have to pay any duty on it. We will mark it 'Christmas Gift' and keep our fingers crossed. Anyway, we hope you will like it and accept it with our sincere best wishes for Christmas and the coming year.

My name is certainly not of Welsh origin. As it is pronounced to rhyme with the French word 'Noel,' I think there may be a possibility that it originated in France.

Yours sincerely,

Frank Doel
For MARKS & CO.

Christmas Greetings
and
All Good Wishes for the
New Year
from

| Geo. Martin | Megan Wells | W. Humphries |
| Cecily Farr | Frank Doel | J. Pemberton |

15TH JANUARY, 1952

Miss Helene Hanff
14 East 95th Street
New York 28, New York
U.S.A.

Dear Miss Hanff,

First of all, we were all so glad that you liked the cloth. It gave us a lot of pleasure to send it and it was one little way of thanking you for all your kind gifts over the last few years. You may be interested to know that it was embroidered, quite recently, by an old lady of over eighty who lives in the flat (apartment) next door to me. She lives all by herself and does quite a lot of needlework as a hobby. She does not often part with any of her work, but my wife managed to persuade her to sell this cloth, and I think she also made her a present of some of the dried egg you sent us which helped a lot.

If you must clean your Grolier Bible, we should advise ordinary soap and water. Put a teaspoonful of soda in a pint of warm water and use a soapy sponge. I think you will find this will remove the dirt and you can then polish it with a little lanolin.

J. Pemberton is a lady and the J. is for Janet.

With best wishes from all of us for the coming year.

Faithfully yours,

Frank Doel

20–1–52

Dear Miss Hanff :

For a long time I have wanted to write to you to thank you for my family's share in the wonderful food parcels you've been sending to Marks & Co. Now I have an excuse as Frank tells me you want to know the name and address of the old lady who embroidered your cloth. It was beautiful, wasn't it?

Her name is Mrs. Boulton and she lives next door at No. 36 Oakfield Court. She was thrilled to know that her cloth had crossed the Atlantic and I know she would be delighted to hear how much you admired it.

Thank you for wanting to send us more dried egg, but we still have a bit left to see us through until spring. Some time between April and September we usually manage all right for eggs, as they go off ration for a time and then we do a bit of trading with the tins, as once for a special occasion I traded a tin of dried egg for a pair of nylons. Not quite legal but it does help us to get by!

I will send you snaps of my happy family one of these days. Our oldest girl was twelve last August, by name Sheila, who by the way is my ready-made daughter, as Frank lost his first wife during the war. Our youngest, Mary, was four last week. Last May, Sheila announced at school that she was sending Mummy and Daddy an anniversary card and told the nuns (it's a convent) that we had been married four years. It took a bit of explaining as you can imagine.

I will close this with all good wishes for the New Year and especially a wish that we may see you in England one of these days.

Sincerely,

Nora Doel

36 Oakfield Court
Haslemere Road
Crouch End
London, N. 8

JAN. 29TH, 1952

Dear Miss Hanff :

Thank you very much for your letter, I appreciate your
kindness in telling me the cloth I worked has given you so
much pleasure. I only wish I could do more. I expect Mrs.
Doel has told you I am getting on in years so I am unable to
do as much as I used to. It is always a joy to me when my
work gets into the hands of someone who appreciates it.

I see Mrs. Doel most days, she often speaks of you. Perhaps I may see you if you come to England.

Again thanking you,

Yours very sincerely,

Mary Boulton

Now listen, Maxine –

I just talked to your mother, she says you don't think the show will run another month and she says you took two dozen pairs of nylons over there, so do me a favor. As soon as the closing notice goes up take four pairs of nylons around to the bookshop for me, give them to Frank Doel, tell him they're for the three girls and Nora (his wife).

Your mother says I am NOT to enclose any money for them, she got them last summer at a close-out sale at Saks, they were very cheap and she'll donate them to the shop, she's feeling pro-British.

Wait'll you see what the shop sent me for Christmas. It's an Irish linen tablecloth, the color of thick cream, hand-embroidered in an old-fashioned pattern of leaves and flowers, every flower worked in a different colour and shaded from very pale to very deep, you never saw anything like it. My junk-shop drop-leaf table CERTainly never saw anything like it, i get this urge to shake out my flowing Victorian sleeve and lift a graceful arm to pour tea from an imaginary Georgian teapot, we're gonna play Stanislavski with it the minute you get home.

Ellery raised me to $250 a script, if it keeps up till June *I* may get to England and browse around my bookshop myself. If I have the nerve. I write them the most outrageous letters from a safe 3,000 miles away. i'll probably walk in there one day and walk right out again without telling them who i am.

I fail to see why you did not understand that groceryman, he did *not* call it 'ground ground nuts,' he called it 'ground ground-nuts' which is the only really SENSible thing to call it. Peanuts grow in the GROUND and are therefore GROUND-nuts, and after you take them out of the ground you grind them up and you have *ground* ground-nuts, which is a much more accurate name than peanut butter, you just don't understand English.

XXX

h. hanff

girl etymologist

P.S. Your mother is setting out bravely this morning to look at an apartment for you on 8th Avenue in the 50's because you told her to look in the theatre district. Maxine you know perfectly well your mother is not equipped to look at ANYTHING on 8th Avenue.

SLOTH :

i could ROT over here before you'd send me anything to read. i oughta run straight down to brentano's which i would if anything i wanted was in print.

You may add Walton's Lives to the list of books you aren't sending me. It's against my principles to buy a book I haven't read, it's like buying a dress you haven't tried on, but you can't even get Walton's Lives in a library over here.

You can look at it. They have it down at the 42nd street branch. But not to take *home* ! the lady said to me, shocked. eat it here. just sit right down in room 315 and read the whole book without a cup of coffee, a cigarette or air.

Doesn't matter, Q quoted enough of it so i know i'll like it. anything he liked i'll like except if it's fiction. i never can get interested in things that didn't happen to people who never lived.

what do you do with yourself all day, sit in the back of the store and read? why don't you try selling a book to somebody?

> *MISS Hanff to you.*
> (I'm helene only to my FRIENDS)

p.s. tell the girls and nora if all goes well they're getting nylons for Lent.

14TH FEBRUARY, 1952

Miss Helene Hanff
14 East 95th Street
New York 28, New York
U.S.A.

Dear Helene,

I quite agree it is time we dropped the 'Miss' when writing to you. I am not really so stand-offish as you may have been led to believe, but as copies of letters I have written to you go into the office files the formal address seemed more appropriate. But as this letter has nothing to do with books, there will be no copy.

We are quite at a loss to know how you managed the nylons which appeared this noon as if by magic. All I can tell you is that when I came back from lunch they were on my desk with a note reading: 'From Helene Hanff.' No one seems to know how or when they arrived. The girls are very thrilled and I believe they are planning to write to you themselves.

I am sorry to say that our friend Mr. George Martin who has been so ill for some time passed away in hospital last week. He was with the firm a great number of years, so with that loss and the King dying so suddenly as well, we are rather a mournful crowd at the moment.

I don't see how we can ever repay you for your many kind gifts. All I can say is, if you ever decide to make the trip to England, there will be a bed for you at 37 Oakfield Court for as long as you care to stay.

With best wishes from us all,

Frank Doel

MARCH 3, 1952

Oh my, i do bless you for that Walton's *Lives*. It's incredible
that a book published in 1840 can be in such perfect condition more than a hundred years later. Such beautiful, mellow rough-cut pages they are, I do feel for poor William
T. Gordon who wrote his name in it in 1841, what a crummy
lot of descendants he must have – to sell it to you casually
for nothing. Boy, I'd like to have run barefoot through
THEIR library before they sold it.

fascinating book to read, did you know John Donne eloped
with the boss's highborn daughter and landed in the Tower
for it and starved and starved and THEN got religion, my
word.

Now listen, I'm enclosing a $5 bill, that *Lives* makes me
very dissatisfied with my *Angler* which I bought before I met
you. It's one of those hard-faced American Classics-for-the-
Masses editions, Izaak just hates it, he says he's not going
around looking like THAT for the rest of my life, so use the
extra $2.50 for a nice English *Angler*, please.

you better watch out, i'm coming over there in 53 if ellery
is renewed. i'm gonna climb up that victorian book-ladder
and disturb the dust on the top shelves and everybody's
decorum. Or didn't I ever tell you I write arty murders for
Ellery Queen on television? All my scripts have artistic back-
grounds – ballet, concert hall, opera – and all the suspects
and corpses are cultured, maybe I'll do one about the rare
book business in your honor, you want to be the murderer or
the corpse?

hh

36 Oakfield Court
Haslemere Road
Crouch End
London, N. 8

MARCH 24TH, 1952

Dear Miss Hanff :

I hardly know how to express my thanks and feelings for the lovely box of everything to eat which you have sent me which arrived today. I have never been sent a parcel before. I really don't think you should have done it. I can only say Thank you very much, I certainly will enjoy everything.

It was very kind of you to think of me in this way. I showed them all to Mrs. Doel, she thought they were lovely.

Again Thanking you very much, and best wishes,

Yours very sincerely,

Mary Boulton

17TH APRIL, 1952

Miss Helene Hanff
14 East 95th Street
New York 28, New York
U.S.A.

Dear Helene (you see I don't care about the files any more),

You will be pleased to know we have just purchased a private library which includes a very nice copy of Walton's *Compleat Angler* and hope to have it to send you next week, price approximately $2.25 and your credit balance with us is more than enough to cover it.

Your Ellery Queen scripts sound rather fun. I wish we could have the chance of seeing some of them on our TV over here – it wants livening up a bit (our TV I mean, not your script).

Nora and all here join me in sending our best wishes,

Yours faithfully,

Frank Doel

37 Oakfield Court
Haslemere Road
Crouch End
London, N. 8

SUNDAY, MAY 4TH, 1952

Dear Helene,

Thanks for the parcel of dried egg received on Friday and I was very glad for same, I did mention something about eggs coming off the ration, well it just hasn't happened so the powder was a godsend for our weekend cakes, etc. Frank is taking some to the shop to send to Cecily, as he keeps forgetting to bring home her address. I expect you know she has left the shop and is waiting to join her husband in the East.

I am enclosing a few snaps, Frank says none of them do him justice, he is much better-looking; but we just let him dream.

Sheila was home for a month's break and we have been gadding about a bit to the seaside for day trips and sightseeing and must now pull in our horns a bit, as the cost of transport here is terrific. It is our ambition to have a car but they are so expensive and a decent secondhand one is dearer than a new one. The new ones are being exported and there are so few for the home market some of my friends have been waiting 5 to 7 years for a new car.

Sheila is going to say a 'jolly good prayer' for you so you may get your wish to come to England because the tin of bacon we had from you on Easter Monday was such a treat. So if 'jolly good prayers' are answered you might have a windfall and be able to come and see us soon.

Well, so long for now and thanks once again.

Nora

May 11, 1952

Dear Frank:

Meant to write you the day the *Angler* arrived, just to
thank you, the woodcuts alone are worth ten times the price
of the book. What a weird world we live in when so beautiful
a thing can be owned for life – for the price of a ticket to a
Broadway movie palace, or 1/50th the cost of having one
tooth capped.

Well, if your books cost what they're worth I couldn't
afford them!

You'll be fascinated to learn (from me that hates novels)
that I finally got round to Jane Austen and went out of my
mind over *Pride & Prejudice* which I can't bring myself to
take back to the library till you find me a copy of my own.

Regards to Nora and the wage-slaves.

HH

37 Oakfield Court
Haslemere Road
Crouch End
London, N. 8

24–8–52

Dear Helene :

Here I am again to thank you most gratefully for our share in the wonderful parcels you so kindly sent to Marks & Co. I wish I could send you something in return.

By the way, Helene, this week we have become the proud possessors of a car, not a new one, mind you, but it goes and that's what matters isn't it? Now maybe you will tell us you're paying us a call?

Mrs. Boulton put up two cousins of mine who came down from Scotland for a couple of weeks and they were very comfortable. She bedded them and I fed them. Now if by any chance you can manage the fare to England next year for the Coronation, Mrs. Boulton will see that you have a bed.

Well, I'll say so long for now and send you our best wishes and thanks once again for the meat and eggs.

Your sincerely,

Nora

26TH AUGUST, 1952

Miss Helene Hanff
14 East 95th Street
New York 28, New York
U.S.A.

Dear Helene,

I am writing once again to thank you on behalf of all here for your three very exciting parcels which arrived a few days ago. It is really too good of you to spend your hard-earned cash on us in this way and I can assure you that we do appreciate your kind thoughts of us.

We had about thirty volumes of Loeb Classics come in a few days ago but alas, no Horace, Sappho or Catullus.

I am taking a couple of weeks' holiday commencing September 1, but as I have just bought a car we are completely 'broke' so will have to take things easy. Nora has a sister who lives by the sea so we are hoping she will take pity on us and invite us to stay with her. It is my first car so we are all very thrilled with it – even though it is an old 1939 model. So long as it gets us to places without breaking down too often we shall be quite happy.

With all good wishes,

Frank Doel

SEPTEMBER 18, 1952

Frankie, guess who came while you were away on vacation? SAM PEPYS! Please thank whoever mailed him for me, he came a week ago, stepped out of four pages of some tabloid, three honest navy-blue volumes of him; I read the tabloid over lunch and started Sam after dinner.

He says to tell you he's overJOYED to be here, he was previously owned by a slob who never even bothered to cut the pages. I'm wrecking them, it's the thinnest India paper I ever saw. We call it 'onion skin' over here and it's a good name for it. But heavier paper would have taken up six or seven volumes so I'm grateful for the India. I only have three bookshelves and very few books left to throw out.

I houseclean my books every spring and throw out those I'm never going to read again like I throw out clothes I'm never going to wear again. It shocks everybody. My friends are peculiar about books. They read all the best sellers, they get through them as fast as possible, I think they skip a lot. And they NEVER read anything a second time so they don't remember a word of it a year later. But they are profoundly shocked to see me drop a book in the wastebasket or give it away. The way they look at it, you buy a book, you read it, you put it on the shelf, you never open it again for the rest of your life but YOU DON'T THROW IT OUT! NOT IF IT HAS A HARD COVER ON IT! Why not? I personally can't think of anything less sancrosanct than a bad book or even a mediocre book.

Trust you and Nora had a fine holiday. Mine was spent in Central Park, I had a month's vacation from joey, my dear little dentist, he went on his honeymoon. i financed the honeymoon. Did I tell you he told me last spring I had to have all my teeth capped or all my teeth out? I decided to have them capped as I have got used to having teeth. But the cost is simply astronomical. So Elizabeth will have to ascend the throne without me, teeth are all I'm going to see crowned for the next couple of years.

i do NOT intend to stop buying books, however, you have to have SOMEthing. Will you see if you can find me Shaw's dramatic criticism please? and also his music criticism? I think there are several volumes, just send whatever you can find, now listen, Frankie, it's going to be a long cold winter and I baby-sit in the evenings AND I NEED READING MATTER, NOW DON'T START SITTING AROUND, GO FIND ME SOME BOOKS.

hh

DECEMBER 12, 1952

To 'her friends at 84, Charing Cross Road' :

The Book-Lovers' Anthology stepped out of its wrappings, all gold-embossed leather and gold-tipped pages, easily the most beautiful book I own including the Newman first edition. It looks too new and pristine ever to have been read by anyone else, but it has been : it keeps falling open at the most delightful places as the ghost of its former owner points me to things I've never read before. Like Tristram Shandy's description of his father's remarkable library which 'contained every book and treatise which had ever been wrote upon the subject of great noses.' (Frank ! Go find me *Tristram Shandy* !)

I do think it's a very uneven exchange of Christmas presents. You'll eat yours up in a week and have nothing left to show for it by New Year's Day. I'll have mine till the day I die – and die happy in the knowledge that I'm leaving it behind for someone else to love. I shall sprinkle pale pencil marks through it pointing out the best passages to some booklover yet unborn.

Thank you all. Happy New Year.

Helene

37 Oakfield Court
Haslemere Road
Crouch End
London, N. 8

17–12–52

Dear Helene :

So sorry I have been so long in dropping you a line. I hope you haven't taken it too badly about Adlai. Maybe he will have better luck next time.

Mrs. Boulton says she will gladly put you up next summer if she is still alive, she says, but I don't know of anyone of her age who is more so, I feel sure she will live to be a hundred. Anyway, we can always fix you up somewhere.

Thanks for the good things you sent us for Christmas, you are much too kind, Helene ! – and if those bodies at Marks & Co. don't give you a banquet when you come over next year, well, they deserve to be shot.

I hope you have a lovely Christmas. Cheerio for now and all our best wishes and thanks.

God bless !

Nora

Frankie, you'll DIE when I tell you –

First, enclosed find $3, P-and-P arrived looking exactly as Jane ought to look, soft leather, slim and impeccable.

Now then. Ellery went off the air and I was shuffling around piling up dentist bills and feeling pale when I was invited to write an outline for a TV show which dramatizes incidents from the lives of famous people. So I rushed home and did an outline of an incident from-the-life-of-a-famous-person and sent it in and they bought it and I wrote the script and they liked it and they're gonna give me more work in the fall.

And whaddaya think I dramatized? JOHN DONNE ELOPING WITH THE BOSS'S DAUGHTER out of Walton's Lives. Nobody who watches television has the slightest idea who John Donne was, but thanks to Hemingway *everybody* knows No Man Is An Island, all I had to do was work that in and it was sold.

So that's how John Donne made the 'Hallmark Hall of Fame' and paid for all the books you ever sent me and five teeth.

I plan to crawl out of bed before dawn on Coronation Day to attend the ceremony by radio. Will be thinking of you all.

cheers

hh

11TH JUNE, 1953

Miss Helene Hanff
14 East 95th Street
New York 28, New York
U.S.A.

Dear Helene,

Just a note to let you know that your parcel arrived safely on June 1, just in time for our Coronation Day celebrations. We had a number of friends at home to watch TV on the day, and so the ham was most welcome to provide them with something to eat. It was delicious, and we all drank your health as well as the Queen's.

It was most kind of you to spend your hard-earned money on us like this, and the rest of the staff join me in saying thanks a lot.

With very best wishes,
Yours sincerely,

Frank Doel

Boldmere Road
Eastcote
Pinner
Middlesex

23-9-53

Helene dear,

Am dashing this off to say you must send *nothing at all* to the shop for Christmas, everything is now off rations and even nylons are available in all the better shops. Please save your money as the most important thing after your dentist is your trip to England. Only don't come in '54 as I shall be out of the country, come in '55 when we shall be back and you can stay with us.

Doug writes that our 'call' may come at any moment as we are next in line for married quarters. The children and I are hoping to join him before Christmas. He is well and happy on Bahrein Island in the middle of the Persian Gulf (if you've got an atlas) but will return to the RAF base at Habbaniya in Iraq when our quarters are available and we will join him there, all being well.

Write again soon. Even if I do 'pop off' Mother will forward your letter.

Love and best wishes —

Cecily

DO YOU MEAN TO SIT THERE AND TELL ME
YOU'VE BEEN PUBLISHING THESE MAMMOTH
CATALOGUES ALL THESE YEARS AND THIS IS
THE FIRST TIME YOU EVER BOTHERED TO SEND
ME ONE? THOU VARLET?

Don't remember which restoration playwright called
everybody a Varlet, i always wanted to use it in a sentence.

As it happens, the only thing which MIGHT interest me
is the Catullus, it's not the Loeb Classics but it sounds like it'll
do. If you still have it, mail it and I'll send you the -/6s/2d
as soon as you translate it, Kay and Brian moved to the
suburbs and left me without a translator.

I shall be obliged if you will send Nora and the girls to
church every Sunday for the next month to pray for the con-
tinued health and strength of the messrs. gilliam, reese,
snider, campanella, robinson, hodges, furillo, podres, new-
combe and labine, collectively known as The Brooklyn Dodgers. If they lose this World Series I shall Do Myself In and
then where will you be?

Have you got De Tocqueville's Journey to America?
Somebody borrowed mine and never gave it back. Why is it
that people who wouldn't dream of stealing anything else
think it's perfectly all right to steal books?

Regards to Megan if she's still there. And what's become
of Cecily, is she back from Iraq?

hh

13TH DECEMBER, 1955

Miss Helene Hanff
14 East 95th Street
New York 28, N.Y.
U.S.A.

Dear Helene,

I feel very guilty about not writing to you before this, but you can put it down to a dose of 'flu which kept me away from the shop for a couple of weeks and a sudden rush of work since I came back.

About the Catullus in our catalogue. This was already sold before we received your letter but I have sent you an edition which contains the Latin text with a verse translation by Sir Richard Burton and also a prose translation by Leonard Smithers, printed in large type, and all for $3.78. The binding is not very handsome but it's a good clean copy. We have no edition of De Tocqueville but will keep looking for one for you.

Megan is still here but planning to go to South Africa to live, we are all trying to talk her out of it. We have heard nothing from Cecily Farr since she went out to the East to join her husband, though they were only to be gone a year.

I shall be only too pleased to root for the Brooklyn Dodgers if you will reciprocate with a few cheers for THE SPURS (the Tottenham Hotspur Football Club to the uninitiated), who are at present languishing next to the bottom of the League. However, the season does not finish until next April so they have plenty of time to get themselves out of the mess.

Nora and all here join me in sending our best wishes for Christmas and the New Year.

Sincerely,

Frank Doel

i write you from under the bed where that catullus drove me.

i mean it PASSETH understanding.

Up till now, the only Richard Burton I ever heard of is a handsome young actor I've seen in a couple of British movies and I wish I'd kept it that way. This one got knighted for turning Catullus – caTULLus – into Victorian hearts-and-flowers.

and poor little mr. smithers must have been afraid his mother was going to read it, he likes to KILL himself cleaning it all up.

all right, let's just you go find me a nice plain Latin Catullus, I bought myself a Cassell's dictionary, I'll work out the hard passages by myself.

WILL YOU TELL MEGAN WELLS SHE IS OUT OF HER COTTONPICKING MIND? if she's that bored with civilization why doesn't she just move to a siberian salt mine?

certainly, certainly, glad to root for anything with Hotspur in it.

Have been socking money in the savings bank for next summer, if TV keeps feeding me till then I'm finally coming over, I want to see the shop and St. Paul's and Parliament and the Tower and Covent Garden and the Old Vic and Old Mrs. Boulton.

i enclose a sawbuck for that thing, that catullus, bound in white Limp – mit-white-silk-bookmark-yet, frankie, where do you FIND these things?!

hh

MARKS & CO., Booksellers
84, Charing Cross Road
London, W.C. 2

16TH MARCH, 1956

Miss Helene Hanff
14 East 95th Street
New York 28, N.Y.
U.S.A.

Dear Helene,

I am sorry to have been so long in writing, but until today we have had nothing to send you and I thought it best to wait a decent interval after the Catullus incident before writing.

We have finally managed to find a very nice edition of *Tristram Shandy* with the Robb illustrations, price approximatedly $2.75. We have also acquired a copy of Plato's *Four Socratic Dialogues*, translated by Benjamin Jowett, Oxford, 1903. Would you like this for $1.00? You have a $1.22 credit with us so the balance due on the two books would be $2.53.

We are waiting to hear whether you are finally coming to England this summer. Both the girls are away at school so you will have your choice of beds at 37 Oakfield Court. I am sorry to say that Mrs. Boulton has been taken to a home, it was rather a sad day but at least she will be looked after there.

Sincerely,

Frank Doel

14 East 95th St.
New York City

June 1, 1956

Dear Frank:

Brian introduced me to Kenneth Grahame's *Wind in the Willows* and I have to have this – with the Shepard illustrations please – but DON'T MAIL IT, JUST HOLD IT FOR ME TILL SEPTEMBER and then mail it to the new address.

The sky fell on us in this cozy brownstone, we got eviction notices last month, they're renovating the building. I decided the time had come to get me a real apartment with real furniture, and in my right mind and shaking all over I went around to the construction site of a new building going up over on 2nd Avenue and signed a lease on a 2½ ('bed-sitter') apartment that isn't even there yet. I am now racing around buying furniture and bookshelves and wall-to-wall carpet with all my England money, but all my life I've been stuck in dilapidated furnished rooms and cockroachy kitchens and I want to live like a lady even if it means putting off England till it's paid for.

Meanwhile the landlord thinks we're not moving out fast enough and is encouraging us by firing the super, leaving nobody to give us hot water or take the garbage out, and also by ripping out the mailboxes, the hall light fixtures and (as of this week) the wall between my kitchen and bathroom. all this and the dodgers disintegrating before my very eyes, nobody-knows-the-trouble-i-see.

Oh, the new address:

AFTER SEPTEMBER 1:
305 E. 72nd St., New York, N.Y. 21

MARKS & CO., Booksellers
84, Charing Cross Road
London, W.C. 2

3RD MAY, 1957

Miss Helene Hanff
305 East 72nd Street
New York 21, N.Y.
U.S.A.

Dear Helene,

Prepare yourself for a shock. ALL THREE of the books you requested in your last letter are on the way to you and should arrive in a week or so. Don't ask how we managed it – it's just a part of the Marks service. Our bill is enclosed herewith showing balance due of $5.00.

Two of your friends dropped in to see us a few days ago and now I have forgotten their names – a young married couple and very charming. Unfortunately they only had time to stop and smoke a cigarette as they were off again on their travels next morning.

We seem to have had more American visitors than ever this year, including hundreds of lawyers who march around with a large card pinned to their clothes stating their home town and name. They all seem to be enjoying their trip so you will have to manage it next year.

With best wishes from us all,

Frank

You might have warned us ! We walked into your book-store and said we were friends of yours and were nearly mobbed. Your Frank wanted to take us home for the weekend. Mr. Marks came out from the back of the store just to shake hands with friends-of-Miss-Hanff, everybody in the place wanted to wine and dine us, we barely got out alive.

Thought you'd like to see the house where your Sweet-William was born.

On to Paris, then Copenhagen, home on the 23rd.

Love,

Ginny and Ed

JANUARY 10, 1958

Hey, Frankie –

Tell Nora to bring her address book up to date, your Christmas card just got here, she sent it to 14 e 95th. st.

Don't know whether I ever told you how dearly I love that *Tristram Shandy*, the Robb illustrations are enchanting, Uncle Toby would have been pleased. Now then. In the back, there's a list of other Macdonald Illustrated Classics which includes the Essays of Elia. I'd love to have this in the Macdonald edition – or any nice edition. If it's Reasonable, of course. Nothing's cheap any more, it's 'reasonable.' Or 'sensibly priced.' There's a building going up across the street, the sign over it says :

> 'One and Two Bedroom Apartments
> At Rents That Make Sense.'

Rents do NOT make sense. And prices do not sit around being reasonable about anything, no matter what it says in the ad – which isn't an ad any more, it's A Commercial.

i go through life watching the english language being raped before me face. like miniver cheevy, i was born too late.

and like miniver cheevy i cough and call it fate and go on drinking.

hh

p.s. whatever became of plato's minor dialogues?

11TH MARCH, 1958

Miss Helene Hanff
305 East 72nd Street
New York 21, New York
U.S.A.

Dear Helene,

I must apologize for having taken so long to answer your last letter but we have had rather a hectic time. Nora has been in hospital for the past several months and I have had my hands full at home. She is almost fully recovered and will be coming home in a week or so. It has been a trying time for us but thanks to our National Health Service it hasn't cost us a penny.

About the Macdonald Classics, we do get a few from time to time but have none at the moment. We had several copies of Lamb's *Essays of Elia* earlier on but they were snapped up during the holiday rush. I am off on a buying trip next week and will look out for one for you. Not forgetting the Plato.

We all hope you had a good holiday season and the girls apologize for sending your Christmas card to the old address.

Faithfully yours,

Frank

MAY 7TH, 1958

Dear Helene,

I have to thank you for your two letters, thanks for the offer, Helene, but there is really nothing we need. I wish we had our own bookshop, then we would be able to repay your kindness by sending you a few books.

I am enclosing a few recent snaps of my happy family, I wish they were better but we seem to have given all the best ones to relatives. You will probably notice how very much alike Sheila and Mary are. It is rather noticeable. Frank says that Mary, as she has been growing up, is exactly like Sheila was at the same age. Sheila's mother was Welsh and I hail from the Emerald Isle so they both must resemble Frank but they are better-looking than he is, though of course he won't admit this!

If you knew how much I hate writing you would feel sorry for me. Frank says for one who talks so much I put up a very bad show on paper.

Again thanks for the letters and good wishes.

God bless!

Nora

18TH MARCH, 1959

Miss Helene Hanff
305 East 72nd Street
New York 21, New York
U.S.A.

Dear Helene,

I don't know how to break the bad news, but two days
after offering you the *Shorter Oxford Dictionary* for your
friend, a man came in and bought it when my back was
turned. I have delayed replying to your letter in the hope
that another one would come along, but no luck yet. I am
terribly sorry to disappoint your friend but you can blame
it all on me as I really ought to have reserved it.

We are sending off by Book Post today the Johnson on
Shakespeare, which we happened to have in stock in the
Oxford Press edition with introduction by Walter Raleigh. It
is only $1.05 and your balance with us was more than enough
to cover it.

We are all sorry to hear that your television shows have
moved to Hollywood and that one more summer will bring
us every American tourist but the one we want to see. I can
quite understand your refusal to leave New York for
Southern California. We have our fingers crossed for you
and hope that some sort of work will turn up soon.

Sincerely,

Frank

AUGUST 15, 1959

sir :

   i write to say i have got work.

   i won it. i won a $5,000 Grant-in-Aid off CBS, it's supposed to support me for a year while I write American History dramatizations. I am starting with a script about New York under seven years of British Occupation and i MARVEL at how i rise above it to address you in friendly and forgiving fashion, your behavior over here from 1776 to 1783 was simply FILTHY.

   Is there such a thing as a modern-English version of the Canterbury Tales? I have these guilts about never having read Chaucer but I was talked out of learning Early Anglo-Saxon/Middle English by a friend who had to take it for her Ph.D. They told her to write an essay in Early Anglo-Saxon on any-subject-of-her-own-choosing. 'Which is all very well,' she said bitterly, 'but the only essay subject you can find enough Early Anglo-Saxon words for is "How to Slaughter a Thousand Men in a Mead Hall."'

   She also filled me in on Beowulf and his illegitimate son Sidwith – or is it Widsith? she says it's not worth reading so that killed my interest in the entire subject, just send me a modern Chaucer.

love to nora.

hh

2ND SEPTEMBER, 1959

Miss Helene Hanff
305 East 72nd Street
New York 21, New York
U.S.A.

Dear Helene,

We were all delighted to hear that you've won a Grant-in-Aid and are working again. We are prepared to be broad-minded about your choice of subject matter, but I must tell you that one of the young inmates here confessed that until he read your letter he never knew that England had ever owned 'the States.'

With regard to Chaucer, the best scholars seem to have fought shy of putting him into modern English, but there was an edition put out by Longmans in 1934, the *Canterbury Tales* only, a modernized version by Hill, which I believe is quite good. It is (of course!) out of print and I am trying to find a nice clean secondhand copy.

Sincerely,

Frank

i don't know, frankie –

Somebody gave me this book for Christmas. It's a Giant Modern Library book. Did you ever see one of those? It's less attractively bound than the Proceedings of the New York State Assembly and it weighs more. It was given to me by a gent who knows I'm fond of John Donne. The title of this book is :

The Complete Poetry

&

Selected Prose

of

JOHN DONNE

&

The Complete Poetry

of

WILLIAM BLAKE?

The question mark is mine. Will you please tell me what those two boys have in common? – except they were both English and they both Wrote? I tried reading the Introduction figuring that might explain it. The Introduction is in four parts. Parts I and II include a Professor's life of Donne mit-illustrations-from-the-author's-works-also-criticism. Part III begins – and God knows I quote – :

> When, as a little boy, William Blake saw the prophet Ezekiel under a tree amid a summer field, he was soundly trounced by his mother.

I'm with his mother. I mean, the back of the Lord God or the face of the Virgin Mary, all right – but why the hell would anybody want to see the prophet Ezekiel?

I don't like Blake anyway, he swoons too much, it's Donne I'm writing about, I am being driven clear up the wall, Frankie, you have GOT to help me.

Here I was, curled up in my armchair so at peace with the world, with something old and serene on the radio – Corelli or somebody – and this thing on the table. This Giant Modern Library thing. So I thought :

'I will read the three standard passages from Sermon XV aloud,' you have to read Donne aloud, it's like a Bach fugue.

Would you like to know what I went through in an innocent attempt to read three contiguous uncut passages from Sermon XV aloud?

You start with the Giant Modern Library version, you locate Sermon XV and there they are : Excerpts I, II and III, – only when you get to the end of Excerpt I you discover they have deleted Jezebel off it. So you get down Donne's *Sermons*, Selected Passages (Logan Pearsall Smith) where you spend twenty minutes locating Sermon XV, Excerpt I, because by Logan Pearsall Smith it isn't Sermon XV, Excerpt I, it's Passage *126. All Must Die*. Now that you've found it, you find he also deleted Jezebel so you get down the *Complete Poetry & Selected Prose* (Nonesuch Press) but they didn't happen to Select Jezebel either, so you get down the *Oxford Book of English Prose* where you spend another twenty minutes locating it because in the *Oxford English Prose* it isn't Sermon XV, Excerpt I nor yet *126. All Must Die*, it's Passage *113. Death the Leveller*. Jezebel is there, and you read it aloud but when you get to the end you find it doesn't have either Excerpt II or III so you have to switch to one of the other three books provided you had the wit to leave all three open at the right pages which I didn't.

So break it to me gently : how hard is it going to be to find me John Donne's Complete Sermons and how much is it going to cost?

i am going to bed, i will have hideous nightmares involving huge monsters in academic robes carrying long bloody butcher knives labelled Excerpt, Selection, Passage and Abridged.

yrs,

h. hffffffffffffff

75

5TH MARCH, 1960

Miss Helene Hanff
305 East 72nd Street
New York 21, New York
U.S.A.

Dear Helene,

I have delayed answering your last two letters until I had some good news to report. I have managed to obtain a copy of the Bernard Shaw–Ellen Terry correspondence. It is not a very attractive edition but it is a good clean copy and I thought I had better send it as this is quite a popular book and it might be quite some time before another copy comes along. The price is approximately $2.65 and you have a credit with us of 50 cents.

I am afraid the complete Donne *Sermons* can be had only by buying Donne's *Complete Works*. This runs to more than 40 volumes and would be very expensive if in good condition.

We hope you had a good Christmas and New Year in spite of the Giant Modern Library.

Nora joins me in sending best wishes.

Sincerely,

Frank

MAY 8, 1960

M. De Tocqueville's compliments and he begs to announce his safe arrival in America. He sits around looking smug because everything he said was true, especially about lawyers running the country. i belong to a Democratic club, there were fourteen men over there the other night, eleven of them lawyers. came home and read a couple of newspaper stories about the presidential hopefuls – stevenson, humphrey, kennedy, stassen, nixon – all lawyers but humphrey.

I enclose three bucks, it's a beautiful book and you can't even call it secondhand, the pages weren't cut. Did I tell you I finally found the perfect page-cutter? It's a pearl-handled fruit knife. My mother left me a dozen of them, I keep one in the pencil cup on my desk. Maybe I go with the wrong kind of people but i'm just not likely to have twelve guests all sitting around simultaneously eating fruit.

cheers

hh

FEBRUARY 2, 1961

Frank?

You still there?

　i swore i wouldn't write till i got work.

Sold a story to Harper's Magazine, slaved over it for three weeks and they paid me $200 for it. Now they've got me writing the story of my life in a book. they're 'advancing' me $1,500 to write it and they figure it shouldn't take me more than six months. I don't mind for myself but the landlord worries.

so I can't buy any books but back in October somebody introduced me to Louis the Duke de Saint-Simon in a miserable abridgement, and I tore around to the Society Library where they let you roam the stacks and lug everything home, and got the real thing. Have been wallowing in Louis ever since. The edition I'm reading is in six volumes and halfway through Vol. VI last night I realized I could not supPORT the notion that when I take it back I will have NO louis in the house.

The translation I'm reading is by Francis Arkwright and it's delightful but I'll settle for any edition you can find that you trust. DO NOT MAIL IT! just buy it and let me know what it costs and keep it there and I'll buy it from you one volume at a time.

Hope Nora and the girls are fine. And you. And anybody else who knows me.

Helene

15TH FEBRUARY, 1961

Miss Helene Hanff
305 East 72nd Street
New York 21, N.Y.

Dear Helene,

You will be pleased to know that we have a copy of the *Memoirs of the Duke de Saint-Simon* in stock in the Arkwright translation, six volumes nicely bound and in very good condition. We are sending them off to you today and they should arrive within a week or two. The amount due on them is approximately $18.75 but please don't worry about paying it all at once. Your credit will always be good at Marks & Co.

It was very good to hear from you again. We are all well, and still hoping to see you in England one of these days.

Love from us all,

Frank

MARCH 10, 1961

Dear Frankie –

Enclosed-please-God-please-find a $10 bill, it better get there, not many of those float in here these days but louis wanted me to get him paid off, he got so tired of the dead-beats at court he didn't want to move in with one 270 years later.

Thought of you last night, my editor from Harper's was here for dinner, we were going over this story-of-my-life and we came to the story of how I dramatized Landor's 'Aesop and Rhodope' for the 'Hallmark Hall of Fame.' Did I ever tell you that one? Sarah Churchill starred as Landor's dewy-eyed Rhodope. The show was aired on a Sunday afternoon. Two hours before it went on the air, I opened the New York Times Sunday book review section and there on page 3 was a review of a book called *A House Is Not a Home* by Polly Adler, all about whorehouses, and under the title was the photo of a sculptured head of a Greek girl with a caption reading : 'Rhodope, the most famous prostitute in Greece.' Landor had neglected to mention this. Any scholar would have known Landor's Rhodope was the Rhodopis who took Sappho's brother for every dime he had but I'm not a scholar, I memorized Greek endings one stoic winter but they didn't stay with me.

So we were going over this anecdote and Gene (my editor) said 'Who is Landor?' and I plunged into an enthusiastic explanation – and Gene shook her head and cut in impatiently :

'You and your Olde English books !'

You see how it is, frankie, you're the only soul alive who understands me.

xx

hh

p.s. Gene's Chinese.

MARKS & CO., Booksellers
84, Charing Cross Road
London, W.C. 2

14TH OCTOBER, 1963

Miss Helene Hanff
305 East 72nd Street
New York 21, N.Y.
U.S.A.

Dear Helene,

You will no doubt be surprised to learn that the two volumes of Virgina Woolf's *Common Reader* are on their way to you. If you want anything else I can probably get it for you with the same efficiency and swiftness.

We are all well and jogging along as usual. My eldest daughter Sheila (24) suddenly decided she wanted to be a teacher so threw up her secretarial job two years ago to go to college. She has another year to go so it looks as though it will be a long time before our children will be able to keep us in luxury.

Love from all here,

Frank

9TH NOVEMBER, 1963

Miss Helene Hanff
305 East 72nd Street
New York 21, New York
U.S.A.

Dear Helene,

Some time ago you asked me for a modern version of Chaucer's *Canterbury Tales*. I came across a little volume the other day which I thought you would like. It is not complete by any means, but as it is quite a cheap book and seems to be a fairly scholarly job, I am sending it along by Book Post today, price $1.35. If this whets your appetite for Chaucer and you would like something more complete later on, let me know and I will see what I can find.

Sincerely,

Frank

All right, that's enough Chaucer-made-easy, it has the schoolroom smell of Lamb's Tales from Shakespeare.

I'm glad i read it. i liked reading about the nun who ate so dainty with her fingers she never dripped any grease on herself. I've never been able to make that claim and I use a fork. Wasn't anything else that intrigued me much, it's just stories, I don't like stories. Now if Geoffrey had kept a diary and told me what it was like to be a little clerk in the palace of richard III – THAT I'd learn Olde English for. I just threw out a book somebody gave me, it was some slob's version of what it was like to live in the time of Oliver Cromwell – only the slob didn't LIVE in the time of Oliver Cromwell so how the hell does he know what it was like? Anybody wants to know what it was like to live in the time of Oliver Cromwell can flop on the sofa with Milton on his pro side and Walton on his con, and they'll not only tell him what it was like, they'll take him there.

'The reader will not credit that such things could be,' Walton says somewhere or other, 'but I was there and I saw it.'

that's for me, I'm a great lover of i-was-there books.

i enclose two bucks for the chaucer, that leaves me a credit with you of 65c which is a larger credit than i have anywhere else.

xx

h

MARCH 30, 1964

Dear Frank –

I take time out from a children's history book (my fourth, would you believe?) to ask if you can help a friend. He has an incomplete set of Shaw in what he insists is just called the Standard Edition. It's bound in rust-colored cloth, he says, if that helps. I enclose a list of what he *has*, he wants all the others in the set but if you have more than a few, don't send them all at once. He'll buy them piecemeal, like me he's a pauper. Send them to him direct, to the address on the list. That's 32nd *Avenue* in case you can't read it.

Do you ever hear anything of Cecily or Megan?

best

helene

14TH APRIL, 1964

Miss Helene Hanff
305 East 72nd Street
New York 21, New York
U.S.A.

Dear Helene,

About the Shaw for your friend, the Standard Edition is still available from the publishers, it is bound in the rust-coloured cloth as he describes and I think there are about 30 volumes in the complete set. Used copies seldom come along but if he would like us to send him new copies we shall be glad to do so and could send him three or four volumes a month.

We have not heard from Cecily Farr in some years now. Megan Wells had enough of South Africa in a very short time and did stop in to give us a chance to say I-told-you-so, before going out to try her luck in Australia. We had a Christmas card from her a few years ago but nothing recently.

Nora and the girls join me in sending love,

Frank

4TH OCTOBER, 1965

Miss Helene Hanff
305 East 72nd Street
New York 21, New York
U.S.A.

Dear Helene,

It was good to hear from you again. Yes, we're still here, getting older and busier but no richer.

We have just managed to obtain a copy of E. M. Delafields *Diary of a Provincial Lady*, in an edition published by Macmillan in 1942, a good clean copy, price $2.00. We are sending it off to you today by Book Post with invoice enclosed.

We had a very pleasant summer with more than the usual number of tourists, including hordes of young people making the pilgrimage to Carnaby Street. We watch it all from a safe distance, though I must say I rather like the Beatles. If the fans just wouldn't scream so.

Nora and the girls send their love,

Frank

SEPTEMBER 30, 1968

Still alive, are we?

I've been writing American history books for children for four or five years.   Got hung up on the stuff and have been buying American history books – in ugly, cardboardy American editions, but somehow I just didn't think the stately homes of England would yield nice English editions of James Madison's stenographic record of the Constitutional Convention or T. Jefferson's letters to J. Adams or like that.

Are you a grandfather yet? Tell Sheila and Mary their children are entitled to presentation copies of my *Collected Juvenile Works*, THAT should make them rush off and reproduce.

I introduced a young friend of mine to *Pride & Prejudice* one rainy Sunday and she has gone out of her mind for Jane Austen. She has a birthday round about Hallowe'en, can you find me some Austen for her? If you've got a complete set let me know the price, if it's expensive I'll make her husband give her half and I'll give her half.

Best to Nora and anybody else around.

Helene

MARKS & CO., Booksellers
84, Charing Cross Road
London, W.C. 2

16TH OCTOBER, 1968

Miss Helene Hanff
305 East 72nd Street
New York City, N.Y. 10021
U.S.A.

Dear Helene,

Yes, we are all very much alive and kicking, though rather exhausted from a hectic summer, with hordes of tourists from U.S.A., France, Scandinavia, etc., all buying our nice leather-bound books. Consequently our stock at the moment is a sorry sight, and with the shortage of books and high prices there is little hope of finding any Jane Austen for you in time for your friend's birthday. Perhaps we will be able to find them for her for Christmas.

Nora and the girls are fine. Sheila is teaching, Mary is engaged to a very nice boy but there is little hope of them getting married for some time as neither has any money! So Nora's hopes of being a glamorous grandmother are receding fast.

Love,

Frank

MARKS & CO., Booksellers
84, Charing Cross Road
London, W.C. 2

8TH JANUARY, 1969

Miss H. Hanff
305 E. 72nd Street
N.Y. 10021
U.S.A.

Dear Miss,

I have just come across the letter you wrote to Mr. Doel on the 30th of September last, and it is with great regret that I have to tell you that he passed away on Sunday the 22nd of December, the funeral took place last week on Wednesday the 1st of January.

He was rushed to hospital on the 15th of December and operated on at once for a ruptured appendix, unfortunately peritonitis set in and he died seven days later.

He had been with the firm for over forty years and naturally it has come as a very great shock to Mr. Cohen, particularly coming so soon after the death of Mr. Marks.

Do you still wish us to try and obtain the Austens for you?

Yours faithfully,
p.p. MARKS & CO.

Joan Todd (Mrs.)
Secretary

Dear Helene,

Thank you for your very kind letter, nothing about it at all offends me. I only wish that you had met Frank and known him personally, he was the most well-adjusted person with a marvellous sense of humour, and now I realize such a modest person, as I have had letters from all over to pay him tribute and so many people in the book trade say he was so knowledgeable and imparted his knowledge with kindness to all and sundry. If you wish it I could send them to you.

At times I don't mind telling you I was very jealous of you, as Frank so enjoyed your letters and they or some were so like his sense of humour. Also I envied your writing ability. Frank and I were so very much opposites, he so kind and gentle and me with my Irish background always fighting for my rights. I miss him so, life was so interesting, he always explaining and trying to teach me something of books. My girls are wonderful and in this I am lucky. I suppose so many like me are all alone. Please excuse my scrawl.

With love,

Nora

I hope some day you will come and visit us, the girls would love to meet you.

Dear Katherine –

I take time out from housecleaning my bookshelves and sitting on the rug surrounded by books in every direction scrawl you a Bon Voyage. I hope you and Brian have a ball in London. He said to me on the phone : 'Would you go with us if you had the fare?' and I nearly wept.

But I don't know, maybe it's just as well I never got there. I dreamed about it for so many years. I used to go to English movies just to look at the streets. I remember years ago a guy I knew told me that people going to England find exactly what they go looking for. I said I'd go looking for the England of English literature, and he nodded and said : 'It's there.'

Maybe it is, and maybe it isn't. Looking around the rug one thing's for sure : it's here.

The blessed man who sold me all my books died a few months ago. And Mr Marks who owned the shop is dead. But Marks & Co. is still there. If you happen to pass by 84 Charing Cross Road, kiss it for me! I owe it so much.

Helene

OCTOBER, 1969

Dear Helene,

This is correspondent No. 3 of the Doel family speaking!
First, may I apologize for the long silence. Believe me, you
were often in our thoughts, we just never seemed to get
around to committing those thoughts to paper. And then
today we got your second letter, and were so ashamed of ourselves that we're writing immediately.

We're pleased to hear about your book and very willingly
give permission to publish the letters.

We are now in our lovely new home. But although we love
the house, and are very happy we moved, we often think of
how much my father would have enjoyed it.

It's futile to have regrets. Although my father was never
a wealthy or powerful man, he was a happy and contented
one. And we're happy that this was so.

We all lead busy lives – perhaps it's better so. Mary works
hard at the University library, and for relaxation goes on car
rallies which last all night. I'm studying part time for a
degree as well as teaching full time, and Mum – she never
stops! So I'm afraid we're very bad correspondents – though
delighted, of course, to receive letters. Nevertheless, we will
try to write when we can if you would like this, and look
forward to hearing from you.

Yours truly,

Sheila

Helene Hanff has been writing letters all her life but in addition she has studied playwriting at the Theatre Guild, written for 'The Hallmark Hall of Fame' and 'Ellery Queen', and has been elected the first woman president of the Lenox Hill Democratic Club. She has written many books for children as well as articles for the *New Yorker* and *Harpers* magazines. Her most recent book is THE MOVERS AND SHAKERS : *The Young Activists of the Sixties.*

The
Duchess
of
Bloomsbury
Street

UP, UP AND AWAY

Theoretically, it was one of the happiest days of my life. The date was Thursday, June 17, 1971; the BOAC lifted from Kennedy airport promptly at 10 A.M.; the sky was blue and sunny, and after a lifetime of waiting I was finally on my way to London.

But I was also fresh out of the hospital after unexpected surgery I was terrified of going abroad by myself (I am terrified of going to Queens or Brooklyn by myself; I get lost) and I had no idea what I would do if something went wrong and nobody met the plane. I especially didn't know how I would manage the mammoth borrowed suitcase I couldn't budge, let alone carry.

Year after year I'd planned a pilgrimage to London, only to have it canceled at the last minute by some crisis, usually financial. This time it was different. From the beginning, heaven seemed to favor the trip.

I'd written a book called *84, Charing Cross Road*, and a few months after it came out in New York, a London publisher named André Deutsch bought it for publication in England. He wrote me that the London edition would be brought out in June and he wanted me there to help publicize the book. Since he owed me a small 'advance,' I wrote and told him to keep the money in his office for me. I figured it was enough to keep me in London for three weeks if I was frugal.

In March, the *Reader's Digest* bought an article I wrote about my fan mail and the *Digest* check bought the BOAC ticket, some expensive clothes and – as things turned out – an expensive surgeon.

With the surgery, contributions came in from all over. The Democratic Club I belong to didn't send flowers to the hospital, they sent a Harrods gift certificate. A friend just back from London stuck a wad of British pounds under my door

99

labeled 'For theatre tickets.' And one of my brothers stopped by and gave me a hundred dollars 'to go to Paris with.' I had no intention of going to Paris (I never wanted to see any city but London) but the hundred meant an extra week in London plus a few frills like cabs and hairdressers. So financially I was all set.

The night before I left, two friends gave me a farewell party. I'd spent the day packing, to the indignant fury of all my vital organs, and I left the party early and was in bed and asleep by midnight. At 3 A.M. I came staring awake, with my insides slamming around and a voice in my head demanding :

'What are you *doing*, going three thousand miles from home by yourself, you're not even HEALTHY !'

I got out of bed, had hysterics, a martini and two cigarettes, got back in bed, and whiled away the rest of the night composing cables saying I wasn't coming.

Paul, the doorman, drove me to the airport. I got on the passport line holding my coat, scarf, magazines and an extra sweater in one hand, while the other held up the pants of my new navy pantsuit which had refused to stay up by themselves since the operation.

Standing on line proved to be no more uncomfortable than hanging by my thumbs, and when I was finally allowed to board the plane I slid into my seat by the window blissful in the knowledge that for five hours I wouldn't have to move a muscle. Somebody brought me sandwiches and coffee I hadn't had to make; somebody brought me a martini; and somebody else was going to clean it all up afterwards. I began to relax.

When I was completely relaxed, the voice in my head inquired what I planned to do if something went wrong and nobody met the plane. To forestall panic, I got the letters out of my shoulder bag and read them over. Those letters were my lifeline.

The first was from Carmen, André Deutsch's publicity girl.

Dear Helene,

I've confirmed your reservation for June 17th at the Kenilworth Hotel. It's just up the way from Deutsch's so you won't feel too alone. The publication date of your book is June 10th, sorry you'll miss it but glad you're on the mend.

We're all looking forward to seeing you on the 18th.

Thanks to a mix-up I had two hotel rooms, one at the Kenilworth and one at the Cumberland. On the advice of well-traveled friends I'd hung onto both rooms in case one wasn't there for me when I arrived. But I was going to the Kenilworth first; it was cheaper.

The second letter was a hasty, last-minute scrawl from Nora Doel. *84, Charing Cross Road* is the story of my twenty-year correspondence with Marks & Co., a London bookshop, and particularly with its chief buyer, Frank Doel, whose sudden death had given rise to the book. Nora is his widow; Sheila is his daughter.

Helene –

Sheila and I will be at Heathrow Airport on Thursday night at ten. We're both very excited.

Have a good trip.

Nora

The third letter was from an Englishman who had written me a fan letter after he read *84, Charing Cross Road* and had asked when I was finally coming to London. I wrote and told him, and he wrote back :

I am a retired publisher now working at London Airport. Please, if I can be of help, USE ME ! I can meet you off your plane and see you through Customs and Immigration. Any friends meeting you would have to meet you AFTER you leave Customs. I would meet you off the plane before your dainty feet touched British soil.

I hadn't the slightest idea how he expected to manage it but I was counting heavily on his getting my dainty feet off the plane. What did I know about Customs and Immigration?

There was a fan letter from the wife of an American professor working at Oxford for a year, inviting me to visit them at Oxford. There was a fan letter from an American living in London who wanted to take me on a walking tour. And there was a letter from Jean Ely, a retired actress in New York whom I'd met as a result of the book:

> Dear Helene:
> I've written to a friend in London about you. He's an Old Etonian who knows London better than anyone I ever met. I've never imposed on him in this way before but I wrote him you were one visitor he must take on a tour of London. His name is Pat Buckley. He'll get in touch with you at the Kenilworth.
> I won't tell you to have a wonderful time, you couldn't possibly have anything else.
>
> Jean
>
> P.S. Keep a diary. So much will be happening to you, you won't remember it all without a diary.

I read all the letters over several times. I checked my passport and vaccination certificate several times; I studied an English Coins card somebody had given me, and I read a BOAC booklet I hadn't had time to read before, on What to Take With You on the Trip. It listed twenty-three items, fourteen of which I didn't have:

3 washable dresses
2 vests
2 pair gloves
small hat(s)
twin set
wool stole
evening dress
evening bag
evening shoes
girdle.

I'd brought three pantsuits, two skirts, several sweaters and blouses, a white blazer and one dress. The dress was silk, chic and expensive, it had a matching coat and was intended to cover large evenings.

I got out my Visitors' Map of London and pored over it. I can read maps only in terms of Up, Down, Left and Right, but I'd marked key places – St. Paul's, Westminster Abbey, the Tower of London – and I'd charted walking tours all over the map. The key places would have to wait till the end of my stay, when I hoped to be able to stand still for long periods, but meanwhile I could walk the city end to end. (I'd discovered I was all right as long as I kept moving.)

I was perfectly calm and happy until a voice announced over the intercom that it was 9:50 P.M. British time, we would be landing at Heathrow Airport in five minutes and it was raining in London.

'Don't panic,' I told myself. 'Just decide *now* what you'll do if Nora and Sheila aren't there and that nut at the airport forgot this is the day you're coming.'

I decided I would look up Nora and Sheila Doel in the phone book and call them. If they didn't answer I would look up Carmen of Deutsch's. If she didn't answer I would go up to an airport official and say:

'Excuse me, sir. I have just arrived from New York, I have a suitcase I can't budge, I don't know where the Kenilworth Hotel is and I am Not Well.'

The plane began its descent and the passengers moved about, collecting hand luggage. I had no hand luggage. I sat frozen and told myself that if nobody met me I would sit in the airport till the next plane left for New York and fly home. At which moment the voice spoke again into the intercom:

'Will Miss Hanff please identify herself to a member of the staff?'

I leaped to my feet and held up my free hand (one hand being permanently attached to the pants) only to find there wasn't a member of the staff in sight. The other passengers, lining up to leave the plane, stared at me curiously as, red-faced but awash with relief, I gathered up everything in my free hand and got on the end of the line. Now that I knew I was being met, I was giddy and half drunk with excitement. I had never really expected to make it to London – and I'd made it.

I reached the stewardess who was saying goodbye to disembarking passengers, and told her I was Miss Hanff. She pointed to the bottom of the ramp and said:

'The gentleman is waiting for you.'

And there he was, a big, towering Colonel Blimp with a beaming smile on his face and both arms outstretched, waiting to get my dainty feet onto British soil. As I went down the ramp to meet him, I thought:

'Jean was right. Keep a diary.'

There's a radio in the headboard of this bed, the BBC just bid me goodnight. The entire radio system here goes to bed at midnight.

Arrival triumphant.

'Helene, my dear!' boomed the Colonel, stooping to kiss me on the cheek, nobody would have believed he'd never set eyes on me before. He's a beaming giant of a man with tufted gray eyebrows and tufted white sideburns, and a vast stomach that marches on ahead of him; and he strode off to see to my suitcase ramrod straight, a Sahib out of Kipling's Old Injah. He came back, followed by a porter with the suitcase on a trolley, put an arm around me and walked me past the Immigration and Customs tables, calling genially to the men behind them, 'Friend of mine!' and that was all I saw of Immigration and Customs.

'Now then,' he said. 'Are you being met?'

I told him Nora and Sheila Doel were there somewhere.

'What do they look like?' he asked, scanning the crowd jammed behind a rope that cordoned off the arrival area.

'I have no idea,' I said.

'Have they a snapshot of you?' he asked.

'No,' I said.

'Do they know what you're wearing?' he asked.

'No,' I said.

'But my dear girl!' he boomed. 'How did you expect to find them?! Wait here.'

He parked me in front of an Information Desk and strode off. A moment later, a voice over the public-address system asked Mrs. Doel to come to the Information Desk – and a pretty, black-haired woman ducked under the cordon directly in front of me, thrust a sheaf of roses in my arms and kissed me.

'Sheila said it was you!' said Nora in a rich Irish brogue. 'We saw every woman off the plane. I said, "That one's too blond," and, "That one's too common." Sheila just kept sayin', "It's the little one in the blue trouser suit, she looks so excited." '

The Colonel steamed up and got introduced, and we went out to Nora's car. She and Sheila got in front, I got in back and the Colonel announced he would follow in his car, unless Sheila would rather he led? Did she know the way to the Cumberland?

'The Kenilworth,' I corrected. I explained about the two hotel rooms and the Colonel stared at me in horror.

'Well, in that case,' he bellowed, 'some total stranger at the Cumberland has a roomful of beautiful roses!'

He drove off to the Cumberland to reclaim his roses and I drove off toward the Kenilworth with Nora's roses in my arms, thinking, 'It was roses, roses, all the way,' and trying to remember who wrote it.

It was dark and rainy as we drove along a highway that might have been any highway leading to any city, instead of the road to the one city I'd waited a lifetime to see. Nora was lecturing me for not staying with her and Sheila in North London ('Frank always meant you to stay with us!'), and as we entered London both of them pointed out the sights:

'There's Piccadilly!'

'This is the West End.'

'This is Regent Street.' And finally, from Sheila:

'You're on Charing Cross Road, Helene!'

I peered out at the darkness, wanting to say something appropriate, but all I could see were narrow wet streets and a few lighted dress-shop windows, it could have been downtown Cleveland.

'I'm here,' I said. 'I'm in London. I made it.' But it wasn't real.

We drove on to Bloomsbury and found the Kenilworth on the corner of a dark street. It's an old brownstone with a shabby-genteel lobby, it's going to suit me.

I registered and the young desk clerk handed me some mail, and then Nora and Sheila and I rode up to inspect Room 352. It looked pleasant and cheerful with the drapes drawn against the rain. Nora surveyed it judiciously from the doorway and announced:

'It's gawjus, Helen.'

'My name's Helene,' I said.

She looked surprised but unimpressed.

'I've been calling you "Helen" for twenty years,' she said, peering into the bathroom. It has a shower stall but no tub. 'Look at this, Sheila, she's got her own loo!'

The loo is the toilet, Sheila thinks it comes from Waterloo.

We went back down and found the Colonel fuming in the sleepy lobby: he'd found his roses lying half dead on the Cumberland Package Room floor and had had a row with the management.

We went into the dining room, empty but still open, and the Colonel located a young Spanish waiter who said his name was Alvaro and allowed we could have sandwiches and tea-or-coffee.

'You smoke too much, Helen,' Nora announced, after we ordered.

'I know it,' I said.

'You're too thin,' she went on. 'I dunno what kind of bloke that surgeon is, to let you come away so soon after your op. A hysterectomy is a very serious op.'

'Is it, Mum,' said Sheila mildly in her university accent. She and Nora exchanged a look, and Nora giggled. They're remarkable, they talk in code and finish each other's sentences, you'd never guess they were stepmother and daughter. Sheila's an attractive girl in her twenties, laconic and unruffled. ('Just like Frank,' Nora told me.)

Nora was much struck by the fact that she and the Colonel were both widowed two years ago. He has one child, a daughter who's being married in the country on Saturday.

'Now, why don't you three girls put on your prettiest dresses and come to the wedding?' he invited expansively. 'It's going to be a superb wedding'

I declined and Nora obviously didn't think she should go if I didn't, so she declined, too, wistfully. ('I don't know him, Helen,' she said when I got her alone. And I said: 'Who knows him?!')

They left at eleven. Nora said she would give me tomorrow to rest and would call me Saturday about the interview. ('We're being interviewed together by the BBC! You've made us all famous!')

The Colonel said he'd be in the country for a week and would call me when he got back and 'arrange a little trip into our glorious countryside.'

I came up and unpacked a few things and climbed into bed with the mail.

Postcard from Eddie and Isabel, old friends from back home. They'll be in town Monday and will pick me up to go sight-seeing.

A note from Carmen at Deutsch's:

Welcome!

I know you're going to be very tired but I'm afraid we have a journalist from the Evening Standard along to see you here at 10 A.M. tomorrow. Someone will be by to pick you up before 10.

On Saturday at 2:30, the BBC want to interview you and Mrs. Doel on 'The World This Weekend.'

On Monday at 3:30 an interview on 'The Woman's Hour,' also at Broadcasting House.

On Tuesday, visits to bookshops, including Marks & Co. (closed but still standing, and we want photos of you there), and at 2:30 an Autograph Party next door at 86 Charing Cross Road, Poole's Bookshop.

On Tuesday evening, André Deutsch will give a dinner for you to meet the Deutsch officers and a distinguished journalist.

I just got uneasy about remembering all those dates, and got out of bed and made a day-to-day calendar out of a pocket memo book. I'm also uneasy about how I'm going to break the news to Carmen that I don't have my picture taken. I'm neurotic, I don't like my face.

I lie here listening to the rain, and nothing is real. I'm in a pleasant hotel room that could be anywhere. After all the years of waiting, no sense at all of being in London. Just a feeling of letdown, and my insides offering the opinion that the entire trip was unnecessary.

The alarm clock went off at eight and I got out of bed and went to the window to see if it was still raining. I pulled back the drapes – and as long as I live I'll never forget the moment. From across the street a neat row of narrow brick houses with white front steps sat looking up at me. They're perfectly standard eighteenth- or nineteenth-century houses, but looking at them I knew I was in London. I got light-headed. I was wild to get out on that street. I grabbed my clothes and tore into the bathroom and fought a losing battle with the damnedest shower you ever saw.

The shower stall is a four-foot cubicle and it has only one spigot, nonadjustable, trained on the back corner. You turn the spigot on and the water's cold. You keep turning, and by the time the water's hot enough for a shower you've got the spigot turned to full blast. Then you climb in, crouch in the back corner and drown. Dropped the soap once and there went fifteen dollars' worth of hairdresser down the drain, my shower cap was lifted clear off my head by the torrent. Turned the spigot off and stepped thankfully out – into four feet of water. It took me fifteen minutes to mop the floor using a bathmat and two bath towels, sop-it-up, wring-it-out, sop-wring, sop-wring. Glad I shut the bathroom door or the suitcase would have been washed away.

After breakfast, I went out in the rain to look at those houses. The hotel is on the corner of Great Russell and Bloomsbury Streets. It fronts on Great Russell, which is a commercial street; the houses I saw from my window are on Bloomsbury.

I walked slowly along the street, staring across it at the houses. I came to the corner, to a dark little park called Bedford Square. On three sides of it, more rows of neat, narrow brick houses, these much more beautiful and beautifully cared for. I sat on a park bench and stared at the houses. I was shaking. And I'd never in my life been so happy.

All my life I've wanted to see London. I used to go to

English movies just to look at streets with houses like those. Staring at the screen in a dark theatre, I wanted to walk down those streets so badly it gnawed at me like hunger. Sometimes, at home in the evening, reading a casual description of London by Hazlitt or Leigh Hunt, I'd put the book down suddenly, engulfed by a wave of longing that was like homesickness. I wanted to see London the way old people want to see home before they die. I used to tell myself this was natural in a writer and booklover born to the language of Shakespeare. But sitting on a bench in Bedford Square it wasn't Shakespeare I was thinking of; it was Mary Bailey.

I come of very mixed ancestry, which includes an English Quaker family named Bailey. A daughter of that family, Mary Bailey, born in Philadelphia in 1807, was the only ancestor I had any interest in when I was a little girl. She left a sampler behind, and I used to stare at that sampler, willing it to tell me what she was like. I don't know why I wanted to know.

Sitting in Bedford Square I reminded myself that Mary Bailey was born in Philadelphia, died in Virgina and never saw London. But the name persisted in my head. Maybe she was a namesake. Maybe it was her grandmother or great-grandmother who had wanted to go home again. All I knew, sitting there, was that some long-dead Mary Bailey or other had finally found a descendent to go home for her.

I came back here and fixed myself up so I'd make a good impression on Deutsch's. Brushed my navy suit jacket (which they will flatly refuse to believe back home) and spent half an hour tying my new red-white-and-blue scarf in an ascot so I'd look British. Then I went down to the lobby and sat bolt upright in a chair by the door, afraid to move for fear of mussing myself, till a young secretary blew in to escort me three doors up Great Russell Street to Deutsch's.

I met Carmen — very brisk and efficient and dramatic-looking — and got interviewed by a bouncy young reporter from the *Evening Standard* named Valerie Jenkins. After the interview the three of us and a photographer piled into a cab, and Carmen said to the driver:

'Eighty-four Charing Cross Road.'

I felt unreal, knowing I was on my way to that address. I'd bought books from 84 Charing Cross Road for twenty years. I'd made friends there whom I never met. Most of the books I bought from Marks & Co. were probably available in New York. For years, friends had advised me to 'try O'Malley's,' 'try Dauber & Pine.' I'd never done it. I'd wanted a link with London and I'd managed it.

Charing Cross Road is a narrow, honky-tonk street, choked with traffic, lined with second-hand bookshops. The open stalls in front were piled with old books and magazines, here and there a peaceful soul was browsing in the misty rain.

We got out at 84. Deutsch's had stuffed the empty window with copies of the book. Beyond the window the shop interior looked black and empty. Carmen went next door to Poole's and got the key and let us into what had once been Marks & Co.

The two large rooms had been stripped bare. Even the heavy oak shelves had been ripped off the walls and were lying on the floor, dusty and abandoned. I went upstairs to another floor of empty, haunted rooms. The window letters which had spelled Marks & Co. had been ripped off the window, a few of them were lying on the window sill, their white paint chipped and peeling.

I started back downstairs, my mind on the man, now dead, with whom I'd corresponded for so many years. Halfway down I put my hand on the oak railing and said to him silently :

'How about this, Frankie? I finally made it.'

We went outside – and I stood there and let them take my picture as meekly as if I did it all the time. That's how anxious I am to make a good impression and not give anybody any trouble.

When I came back to the hotel there was a letter at the desk. From Pat Buckley, the Old Etonian Jean Ely wrote to about me.

No salutation, just :

Jean Ely writes that you are here on your first visit. Can you have a bit of supper here on Sunday at 7 :30? – and we will drive around and see a bit of old London.

Call me Saturday or Sunday before 9 :30 A.M.

In haste –

P.B.

Totally demoralized.

Just came up from breakfast and phoned Pat Buckley.

'Oh yes,' he said in a very U accent, 'Hallo.'

I told him I'd love to come to supper tomorrow night and asked if there were other people coming.

'I'm not giving a supper party for you' he said impatiently. 'Jean wrote me you wanted to see London!'

I stammered that I was glad we'd be alone, I'd only asked so I'd know how to dress; if we were alone I could wear a pantsuit.

'Oh, Lord, must you?' he said. 'I loathe women in trousers. I suppose it's old-fashioned of me but I do think you all look appalling in them. Oh well, I suppose if you must, you must.'

It's fifty degrees here and raining, I'm not climbing into a summer skirt for him.

Nora just phoned, she'll pick me up at two this afternoon for the interview.

'You're right behind the British Museum, Helen,' she said. 'Go sit in the Reading Room, it's very restful.'

Told her I see enough museums in New York, and God knows I sit in enough Reading Rooms.

Will now slog out in the wet and tour Bloomsbury.

MIDNIGHT

Nora and I were interviewed at Broadcasting House, it's the only big modern building I've seen and I hope I don't see another one; it's a monstrosity – a huge semicircular block of granite, it looks obese. They don't understand sky-scrapers here. In New York they don't understand anything else.

The interviewer was choice. First she told the radio audience that though Nora and I had corresponded over a twenty-year period we'd never met. Then she turned to us and asked us what we thought of each other : now that we'd met, were we disappointed? If we'd never corresponded and had just met, would we like each other?

'Now what kind of question was that to ask me?' Nora demanded when we came out. 'How-would-I-like-you-if-we'd-just-been-introduced. How do I know whether I'd have liked you or not? I've known you for twenty years, Helen!'

She drove me out Portland Place and through the Regent's Park section, which I loved passionately on sight. We passed Wimpole Street and Harley Street – and there I was in a *car*, I felt as if I were locked in a metal container and couldn't get out, but it was raining. I'm going back there on foot the first dry day.

There's a Crescent of Nash houses – I'm not too clear about when Nash lived but he built tall white opulent houses reeking of Beau Brummell and Lady Teazle – and when the rain stopped for a little we got out of the car and sat on a park bench so I could stare at the Crescent. We chose which houses we'll buy if we're born rich next time.

Nora told me she came to London as a poor servant girl from Ireland before the war. She worked in one of the houses of the gentry as a kitchen maid, cutting paper-thin bread for the cucumber sandwiches.

She drove me home to Highgate for dinner. She and Sheila bought a house out there after Frank died and the younger daughter married. We drove past Hampstead Heath on the way, and Nora stopped the car at the cemetery where Karl Marx is buried. The gates were locked but I peered over the wall at him.

Their house is high in the hills of North London on an attractive suburban street that blazes with roses, every house had a rose garden in full bloom. The roses here are as wildly colored as a New England autumn : not just red, pink and yellow, but lavender roses, blue roses, purple and orange roses. Every color has a separate fragrance, I went berserk smelling my way around Nora's garden.

We had strawberries and thick English cream for dessert, and when Nora came to her last berry she looked up at Sheila, stricken, and said :

'It came out "never" again, Sheila!'

She eats berries to the old children's rhyme to find out when she's going to marry again: 'This year, next year, sometime, never.' When it comes out 'never,' Sheila has to comfort her. Sheila's much more like Nora's mother than her stepdaughter.

Nora cut a fresh armload of roses for me, and Sheila drove me home. She teaches in a suburban school. There are two men who take her out; I think both of them bore her, she still hasn't met one she wants to marry.

Big excitement in the lobby when I came in because of the *Evening Standard* interview; one of the desk clerks had saved a copy for me.

Excerpt:

She steps into London, frightfully trim in a chic navy trouser-suit from Saks and a foulard tied French-style.

Kill yourself tying an ascot and it comes out French-style. Story of my life.

You can't imagine how funny it strikes me when somebody calls me chic. I'm wearing the same kind of clothes I've worn all my life and for years I was looked on as a bohemian mess. My sister-in-law Alice, for instance, used to wear herself out every year trying to find a shoulder bag to give me for Christmas because I wouldn't carry a handbag and nobody else wore shoulder bags so no manufacturers made them. (Handbags make you choose between your wallet, your glasses and your cigarettes. Choose two of the three and maybe you can get your bag closed.) I also wouldn't wear high heels because I like to walk, and you can't walk if your feet hurt. And I lived in jeans and slacks because skirts are drafty in winter and hamper you when you walk, and besides, if you're wearing pants nobody knows there's a run in one stocking.

So for years I was this sartorial horror who ran around in low heels, pants and shoulder bags. I still run around that way – and after a lifetime of being totally out of it, I'm so With it my pantsuit gets a rave review in the *Evening Standard*.

Sallied forth with my map after breakfast and saw the sights of Bloomsbury. Got lost several times; it seems a street can be on the Left on your map without necessarily being Left of where you're standing. Various gents came out from under umbrellas to point me where I wanted to go.

It cleared after lunch and I'm now in a neighborhood park, lying in a deck chair soaking up the fog. There are three handkerchief-sized parks very close to the hotel. This one's just beyond the British Museum. Sign on the gate says:

RUSSELL SQUARE

PLEASE DON'T LEAVE LITTER

PERSONS WITH DOGS ARE REQUIRED TO KEEP THEM UNDER PROPER CONTROL

There's a rose garden in the middle of the square encircling a very practical birdbath: a marble slab with a thin jet of water in the center. A bird can stand around and drink or wash his feathers without drowning. Wish whoever designed it would go to work on the English shower problem.

An elderly gentleman in uniform just came up, bowed and said:

'Fourpence, please.'

For the use of the deck chair.

He was apologetic about the weather, he and I are the only ones out here. I said the rain was good for the roses, and he told me the gardeners in London's squares compete every year for the honor of growing the best roses.

'I do think this year our chap has a chance,' he said. Told him I would definitely root for the Russell Square gardener.

Have to go put on the navy suit for Pat Buckley. Or I may just be mean and stay in my second-best coffee-brown on account of the weather.

MIDNIGHT

I've been sitting on the edge of the bed for an hour in a complete daze. I told him if I die tonight I'll die happy, it's all here, everything's here.

Pat Buckley lives in Rutland Gate, it's down in Knightsbridge or Kensington below the left-hand edge of my Visitors' Map, I took a cab. Rutland Gate is a small compound of white stone houses round a green square. Everything in London is round a green square, they're like small oases everywhere.

He has a ground-floor flat. I rang the bell and he opened the door and said :

'Hallo, you found it all right.'

He's slight – thin build, thin face, indeterminate age – and he has one of those light, almost brittle, English voices, pleasant but neutral. He took my jacket and ushered me into an Oscar Wilde drawing room. There's a full-length portrait of his mother in her court-presentation gown on one wall. On another wall, a glass cabinet houses his collection of gentlemen's calling-card cases – small square cases, gold, silver, onyx inlaid with pearl, ivory worked with gold filligree, no two alike. The collection is his hobby and it's dazzling.

He brought me sherry, and when I told him I found Eton very glamorous he brought me his Eton class book and showed me photos of his rooms there.

We had supper in the dining room at a polished mahogany table set with heavy English silver. He has a 'daily' who leaves a cold supper for him and his guests and makes the coffee and sets the table before she leaves. The place setting was the same as at home – fork at the left, knife and spoon at the right – but lying horizontally above the dinner plate were an oyster fork and a soup spoon. I let him go first so I could see what you did with them.

We had chicken salad followed by strawberries and cream – and that's what you use them for : you spear a strawberry with the oyster fork, scoop cream up on the soup spoon, transfer the berry to the spoon and slurp.

After supper we climbed into his car. He didn't ask what I wanted to see, he just drove me to the corner where the Globe Theatre stood. Nothing is there now, the lot is empty. I made him stop the car and I got out and stood on that empty lot and I thought the top of my head would come off.

He got out of the car then, and we prowled the dark alleys nearby – Shakespeare's alleys, still there. And Dickens' alleys : he pointed to an Artful Dodger peering furtively out the window of an ancient pile of stone.

He took me to a pub called The George, and as he opened the door for me he said in that light, neutral voice :

'Shakespeare used to come here.'

I mean I went through a door Shakespeare once went through, and into a pub he knew. We sat at a table against the back wall and I leaned my head back, against a wall Shakespeare's head once touched, and it was indescribable.

The pub was crowded. People were standing at the bar and all the tables were full. I was suddenly irritated at all those obtuse citizens eating and drinking without any apparent sense of where they were, and I said snappishly :

'I could imagine Shakepeare walking in now, if it weren't for the people.'

And the minute I said it I knew I was wrong. He said it before I could :

'Oh no. The people are just the same.'

And of course they were. Look again, and there was a blond, bearded Justice Shallow talking to the bartender. Further along the bar, Bottom the Weaver was telling his ponderous troubles to a sharp-faced Bardolph. And at a table right next to us, in a flowered dress and pot-bellied white hat, Mistress Quickly was laughing fit to kill.

He dragged me out of there and drove me to see St. Paul's by floodlight. I wanted at least to walk up the steps and touch the doors of John Donne's cathedral but it will be there tomorrow, there's time, there's time.

He drove me to the Tower of London, more huge and terrifying than I'd imagined, like a sprawling medieval Alcatraz. We got there just at ten, so I could watch the guards lock the Tower gates. For all their flashy black-and-scarlet uniforms, they are grim and frightening as they lock the gates to that dread prison with darkness closing in. You think of the young Elizabeth sitting somewhere behind the stone walls wanting to write and ask Bloody Mary to have her beheaded with a sword instead of an ax.

When the gates were locked, the guards marched back toward the huge iron Tower door. It rose to let them pass through, lowered and clanged shut behind them, and the light voice beside me said :

'They haven't missed a night in seven hundred years.'

The mind boggles. Even going back only three hundred years, you think of London during the Great Fire, the Great Plague, the Cromwell revolution, the Napoleonic wars, the First World War, the Second World War –

'They locked the Tower with all this ceremony,' I asked him, 'every night, even during the Blitz?'

'Oh yes,' he said.

Put THAT on Hitler's tombstone, tell THAT to that great American patriot, Wernher von Braun, whose buzz bombs destroyed every fourth house in London.

When he drove me home and I tried to thank him, he said :

'Oh, thank *you*! Most Americans won't take this tour. They'll drive around with me for a quarter of an hour and then they want to know where the Dorchester Bar is.'

He said most Americans he knows never see London.

'They take a taxi from the Hilton to Harrods, from Harrods to the theatre, from the theatre to the Dorchester Bar.'

He said he knows four American businessmen who've been in London for a week without ever leaving the Hilton.

'They stay shut up in their rooms all day with the telephone and a bottle of Scotch, you wonder why they ever left the States.'

He gave me a list of sights to see but didn't suggest showing them to me himself.

Eddie and Isabel picked me up this morning to go sight-seeing; Isabel is an old school friend, they live in Texas. They are the most conventional, conservative people I know.

It was sunny this morning, and when they came for me the sight of them charmed me : Isabel wore cotton overalls and a print blouse, Eddie was in a sports shirt and slacks. It was the first time I'd ever seen them that they didn't look ultra proper-and-respectable. I had an interview at Broad-casting House at three and I thought I might not get back here first so I wore my marked-down beige linen pantsuit; next to them I was overdressed.

They'd been to London before and had seen the sights so we just wandered around the shopping district all morning. They like to window-shop and buy curios and good prints and we did that. At lunch time, we were wandering along a street when I stopped suddenly and gawked because there, directly ahead of us, was Claridge's.

Claridge's is where all the characters in Noel Coward lunch. For years I've had glamorous images of fashionable London sailing grandly into Claridge's.

Eddie asked what I was staring at and I explained.

'Fine,' he said promptly. 'We'll have lunch at Claridge's.'

It was a spontaneous, generous gesture very typical of him. I waited for Isabel to say, 'Now Eddie, not the way we're dressed !' but to my astonishment, she didn't.

'I think it's very fancy,' I said. 'Let's go home and change first.'

'They'll take our money,' said Eddie dryly – and took our arms and led us proudly into Claridge's.

I'm a slob by nature. On an ordinary day at home I couldn't care less how I look. But this was CLARIDGE'S. I sat through lunch in that room of grace and elegance sur-rounded by tables of perfectly groomed Londoners – sand-wiched between two happy Texans dressed for a picnic and affectionately pleased at having taken me somewhere special.

After lunch they went with me to Broadcasting House, and then more window shopping, and at six we were in the theatre district. A few people were on line at the Aldwych hoping for last-minute return tickets to *A Midsummer Night's Dream*. Eddie spoke to a man on line and came back and said :

'There are always a few returns. If we get on line now, we can get tickets at seven, when the box office opens. It's a seven-thirty curtain, we'll eat afterwards.'

This was the Peter Brook production, you understand, the National Shakespeare Theatre Company production. I would have given a week of my life for a ticket. I'd tried to get them for Nora and Sheila and me through the hotel, it was the one show I couldn't get, it's sold out for the rest of the run. And much as I wanted to see it, I *couldn't* have walked into that theatre looking the way we looked – in clothes we'd worn since early morning and without so much as having washed our faces all day. And Eddie and Isabel, who wouldn't have dreamed of going to the theatre that way in Houston, were ready to do it in London.

The whole thing was academic for me : I couldn't have stood on that line for ten minutes, much less an hour. I'd stood peering in at shop windows most of the day with my teeth gritted and by six I'd had it. I told them I thought I'd call it a day and go sit somewhere before my insides fell out on the pavement. They're old friends, they immediately abandoned the project and we went to dinner at a little side-street pub instead.

Not till I got home did it dawn on me that they and I had completely reversed roles. Coming abroad, where nobody knows them, Eddie and Isabel have rid themselves of a lot of social inhibitions. Coming abroad, where nobody knows me, I've acquired a whole set of inhibitions I never had at home. Wild?

Carmen just phoned to remind me of the Autograph Party tomorrow and the Deutsch dinner tomorrow night. I told her I have a calendar propped against the travelling clock so it's the first thing I see when I turn the alarm off in the morning.

Asked her what I do if nobody shows up for my autograph; she said briskly Talk to the manager, he's a fan. After twenty minutes say you have a headache and he'll get you a cab.

We toured the bookshops in the rain. They all had *84* prominently displayed, and all the managers and sales people bowed and beamed and shook my hand, and after the third bookshop I got terribly poised and gracious about it all, like I was used to it. We got to Poole's at two-thirty for the Autograph Party – and would you believe a long line of people waiting for my important autograph? On a rainy Tuesday?

They'd set up a table for me at the head of the line and I sat down and asked the first man to tell me his name and a bit about himself so I could write something personal, I can*not* break myself of the habit of autographing books with chummy little messages that take up the whole front page.

A lady from California plunked down twelve copies and got out her list and said, This first one's for her brother Arnold in the hospital, could I write something cheerful? and this one's for Mrs. Pratt next door who's watering her plants, and this one's for her daughter-in-law Pat, could I write 'To Pat from Mother Crawford Via—'? Twelve. Now and then I'd squint along the line (I wasn't wearing my glasses, I'm a celebrity) and apologize for keeping everybody waiting; they all just smiled and went on standing patiently, people are unbelievable.

I got nearly to the end of the line and said automatically without looking up, 'Will you tell me your name sir?' and he said, 'Pat Buckley,' meekly, and I looked up and there he was with two books under his arms. I told him I want to give him a copy. I autographed his two for him to give to friends.

He asked whether I'm free on Saturday if he's 'able to arrange a little outing'; I said I'm free for any outing he arranges any day at all, and he beamed and said he'd be in touch.

After the autographing, I had sherry with the manager, Mr. Port. (Fact.) He gave me a letter someone had left there for me and I put it in my shoulder bag and brought it home and just now remembered it and got it out and opened it.

Dear Miss Hanff –

Welcome to England. A benefactor from Philadelphia sent us your book and we love it, as do all our friends.

I wonder if you would be free on Monday next, June 28, and would like to see Peter Brook's production of 'A Midsummer Night's Dream' with us? It is at the National Shakespeare Company's London theatre, the Aldwych. We are taking two Australian friends with us, both devotees of your book.

My husband is English, so am I, but I had an American mother.

We'd love it if you are free to come. Will you telephone me? – and we can plan where to meet and eat first.

Sincerely,

Joyce Grenfell

I feel as if God had leaned down from heaven and pasted a gold star on my forehead.

I'm sitting here all gussied up in the silk cocktail-dress-and-coat for the Deutsch dinner, ready half an hour early as usual. I'm afraid even to smoke, I'll get ashes on it.

1 A.M.

The desk buzzed up when the car came, and when I went down to the lobby, Mr. Otto, the Kenilworth manager, bowed ceremoniously and said :

'Madam's car awaits.'

Told him this was my first and last chance to be a celebrity and I was gonna make the most of it. He nodded solemnly and said : 'Quite.' He and the two boys who work as desk clerks get a charge out of all my roses and phone calls and notes-left-at-the-desk. So do I, believe it.

The dinner party was at a Hungarian restaurant called Victor's. Victor is a close friend of André Deutsch, they're both Hungarian but Victor is more so. He bowed and kissed my hand and told me I was 'beautiful' and 'Queen of London for a month' and my book was also 'beautiful.' I told Deutsch :

'He's straight out of Molnar.'

And Deutsch looked at me in mild surprise and said :

'Oh, did you know Ferenc ?'

No, I didn't know Ferenc but Deutsch did. If any Molnar fan is still alive and reading this, you pronounce it Ference.

The dinner was in a private upstairs dining room; we paraded up the carpeted stairs, about eight of us, and into a dining room, where a large round table was just jumping with wine glasses and flowers and candles. I sat between Deutsch, very old-world and courtly, and the 'distinguished journalist' whose name I didn't get.

Everybody at dinner was bowled over to learn I was going to meet Joyce Grenfell. I know her as a comedienne in British films but she's much more famous over here for her one-man shows, which I never saw. She writes all her own material and the show always sells out. So now of course I'm nervous about meeting her.

Over coffee, somebody passed a copy of *84* around the table for all the guests to sign for me. Above the signatures somebody had written a flowery tribute to 'an author who combines talent with charm' and sociability with something else, and Deutsch read it and nodded vehemently and signed his name and handed the book to me with a flourish. And Victor read it and said Yes, Yes, it was So ! and signed his name ('Your host !') and kissed my hand again, and dessert was a fancy decorated cake with WELCOME HELENE on it in pink icing.

Got home at midnight, swept into the lobby and informed Mr. Otto and the boys at the desk I am hereafter to be known as the Duchess of Bloomsbury. Or Bloomsbury Street, at least.

The two desk clerks are students from South Africa. One of them has to go back in a few days, and the other advised him conversationally:

'If the police come after you, eat my address.'

Nora and I were taken to lunch by a rare-book dealer, and over lunch a bizarre story from Nora.

I gather book dealers are as clannish as actors, and the closest friends Frank and Nora had for ten years were a book dealer named Peter Kroger and his wife, Helen. The Doels and Krogers were inseparable despite the fact that the two men were competitors. One New Year's Eve, the Doels gave a party, and Helen Kroger arrived looking very exotic in a long black evening dress.

'Helen, you look like a Russian spy!' said Nora. And Helen laughed and Peter laughed and a few months later Nora picked up the morning paper and discovered that Helen and Peter Kroger *were* Russian spies.

'All the journalists came swarming round to the house,' Nora told me, 'offering me a couple of thousand quid to tell them about "the ring." I told them the only ring I knew anything about was my wedding ring.'

She visited the Krogers in prison and Peter asked if she remembered telling Helen she looked like a Russian spy.

'It must have given them a turn,' I said.

'I don't know,' said Nora. 'He just asked if I remembered it. Then we talked about something else.'

She and Frank went to the trial and discovered that everything the Krogers had told them about their past lives had been invented. I asked if this bothered her, Nora said No, she understood it.

'They were the best friends we ever had,' she said. 'They were fine people, lovely people. It was all political, I s'pose they had their reasons.'

A year later the Krogers were exchanged for a British spy held by the Russians. They live in Poland now. Helen and Nora still write to each other at Christmas.

Phoned Joyce Grenfell at dinner time, told her what movies I'd seen her in and she said :

'Then you'll know me, I'm the one with the bangs.' I'm to meet them for dinner Monday at the Waldorf, which is next door to the theatre.

I finally got a day to myself and did the Regent's Park area on foot. Walked around the Nash Crescent twenty or thirty times, saw the house on Wimpole Street where Robert Browning came to call on Elizabeth, walked Harley Street – and also Devonshire Street, Devonshire Place, Devonshire Mews, Devonshire Close and Devonshire Mews Close, this is a lovely city.

There was a note at the desk for me when I came back. No salutation.

> Can you be here at twelve noon *sharp* on Saturday? We are driving down to Windsor and Eton and have rather a lot to do.
>
> In haste –
>
> P.B.

We are driving down to Windsor and Eton. Me, this is.

I love the way he never uses a salutation. It always aggravates me, when I'm writing to some telephone-company supervisor or insurance man, to have to begin with 'Dear Sir' when he and I both know nobody on earth is less dear to me.

I'm writing this in the Kenilworth Lounge. Not to be confused with the Kenilworth TV Room, where everybody sits bolt upright on little straight chairs in total darkness staring at some situation comedy. The Lounge is just off the lobby. It's a pleasant room with easy chairs and a sofa, but if you want to write in your journal you have to slither an eye around the door before entering. If there's a woman alone in here she's looking for somebody to talk to. If there are two women already talking, they're gracious and friendly enough to include you in the conversation, and you can't decline to be included without seeming *un*gracious and *un*friendly.

Tonight when I came in there was only a man at the desk

writing letters, he just left. He asked me for a light, and when he heard my American accent he told me he'd lived in New York for a year.

'And then one day I was walking down Fifth Avenue with an American friend and I said to him : "Why are you running?" And he said : "I'm not running!" And then I knew it was time to come home.'

People here ask you for 'a light' only if you're smoking and they can light their cigarette from yours. Nobody would dream of asking you for a match, it would be like asking you for money. Matches are not free over here. There are none in ashtrays in hotel lobbies and none on restaurant tables. You have to buy them at the store, I suppose they're imported and too expensive to fling around the way they're flung around at home.

A lady just came in, she asked Am I the writer? she heard about me at the desk. She lives in Kent, she doesn't care for London, she's here because her brother's in the hospital here but at least she's seeing a bit of Bloomsbury, he just won't hear of her staying in the room all day, so this afternoon she went out to the Dickens House in Doughty Street, have I been there?

She wants to talk so we'll talk.

I got the first week's hotel bill this morning, much steeper than I'd anticipated, what with assorted lunches and dinners and a 12 per cent surcharge added for tips. I just took it up the street to Deutsch's, to Mr. Tammer, their accountant. He's a solemn, bespectacled gentleman who gives you a sudden warm smile when you say hello to him. He'll need it with me around, he's my personal banker. He's got all my 'advance' money in cash in the office safe and he's doling it out to me weekly. He gave me cash to pay the hotel bill and ten pounds, which is my Allowance for the week; when I run short I dip into my brother's hundred. I had ten of the hundred with me for him to change into pounds, and he got out all his charts and machines and figured the latest exchange rate very tensely and meticulously, God forbid he should cheat me out of fifteen cents.

There was a letter for me at Deutsch's which intrigues me, it's from a man I never knew existed. Nobody I corresponded with at Marks & Co. ever mentioned him.

Dear Miss Hanff,

I am the son of the late Ben Marks of Marks & Co. and want you to know how delighted I am that you are here, and how very much my wife and I would like you to dine with us.

I do not know where you are staying so could you please ring me at the above telephone numbers? The second one is an answering service and any message left there will reach me.

We're both looking forward to meeting you.

Sincerely,

Leo Marks

The secretary who gave me the letter told me he called and asked where he could reach me.

'But we never tell anyone where you're staying,' she said. 'We just ask them to get in touch with you through us.'

I took a very dim view of this and went into Carmen's office to straighten it out.

'Carmen, dear,' I said, 'I am not the kind of author who wants to be protected from her public. Any fan who phones might want to feed me, and I am totally available as a dinner guest. Just give out my address all over.'

She said there are at least two interviews to come and she'll make them both over lunch. Some interviewer asked me if I planned 'to buy silver and cashmere here – or just books?' I said I planned to buy *nothing* over here, everything I see in a shop window has a price tag reading 'One Day Less in London.'

Off to Parliament.

MIDNIGHT

I'VE BEEN TO THE OLD VIC, shades of my stage-struck youth, walking into that theatre was a thrill. Nora and Sheila and I saw *Mrs. Warren's Profession.* The theatre has the atmosphere of the old Met in New York and the Academy of Music in Philadelphia; the audience files in with a kind of festive reverence, like people going to church on Christmas Eve.

Sheila had trouble parking the car, she got to the theatre three minutes after the curtain was up and was promptly shunted off downstairs to the lounge to watch the first act on closed-circuit TV, you do not trail down the aisle after Mass has started.

I'll never understand why they did *Mrs. Warren's Profession* in turn-of-the-century costumes. Politicians and businessmen don't own whorehouses any more? Poor girls are not expected to starve virtuously rather than eat un-virtuously any more? Moral pillars of society don't keep mistresses in country cottages any more? Who does such a play as a costume piece belonging to some other era? Bernie Shaw would have a fit.

I asked Nora about Leo Marks, she said she only met him and his wife a few times but 'they seemed a nice young couple.' She said he's a writer.

I'm sitting here eating vitamin C, think I'm getting a cold. Tried reading Mary Baker Eddy once, should've stuck with it.

It finally turned sunny and warm, thank God, so I could wear a skirt for PB. (Headline in the newspaper read ENGLAND SWELTERS IN 75-DEGREE HEAT.) Wore my brown linen skirt and the new white blazer, and he beamed and said, 'You look charming,' and asked if the brown-and-white scarf came from Harrods. (I borrowed it off the cocktail dress.)

He said as we drove that we wouldn't be able to go through Windsor Castle after all, 'the Queen's in residence,' but we would stop at Windsor for sherry with two elderly sisters, he thought I'd find them and their house delightful.

On the way to Windsor there's a Home for Tired Horses. Their owners visit them on Sundays and bring them cream buns.

Windsor is full of casual anachronisms. The sisters live on a seventeenth-century street in one of a row of Queen Anne houses, each with a car parked at the curb and a TV antenna sticking out of the roof. PB parked at the back of the house by the rose garden and we were met there by the dominant sister, who cut a pink rose for me to wear and took us into the house and along a narrow old-fashioned hall to the living room, where the shy sister met us. The shy sister poured sherry and both of them regretfully informed PB that their ghost had gone.

The ghost was living in the house when they bought it twenty years ago and stayed on. He was very quiet and no trouble most of the time. But he liked the house to be lived in, he liked people about; and every time the sisters packed for a trip and made arrangements to close the house, the ghost went berserk with fury. Pictures were knocked off the walls, wine glasses went hurtling off the sideboard and broke, lamps crashed to the floor, pots and pans went clattering and banging round the kitchen all night long. The rampage lasted till the sisters left for their holiday. For twenty years, this happened every time they went up to London during the season or into the country or abroad. This year, for the first time, the sisters made plans to go away, they packed for the trip – and the house remained silent. The pictures and wine glasses and lamps were undisturbed, the kitchen was quiet, the ghost had gone. The sisters were rather sad about it, they'd got fond of him.

One of the sisters took me up to the top-floor bathroom to look out the window. They run up there to see whether the Queen has arrived. From the bathroom window you can see the Windsor Castle flagpole. If the Queen's in residence the flag is flying.

They apologized for not giving us lunch, they were going to watch Philip play polo.

PB and I picnicked on the Windsor lawn. He (or the daily) had packed a basket with three kinds of sandwiches, a thermos of iced tea, peaches and cookies – and after-dinner mints, I love him to death, there's an Edwardian finishing touch to everything he does. Like the china ashtray he keeps on the front ledge of his car, he obviously doesn't care for the tin one that comes built in.

There's a footbridge connecting Windsor and Eton. PB wore his Eton tie, and the gate keeper saw it and said, 'You're an Eton man, sir!' and let us into rooms not open to tourists.

If you're born in the U.S. with a yearning love of classical scholarship and no college education, you are awed by a school in which for centuries boys have learned to read and write Greek and Latin fluently by the time they're in their teens. PB took me into the original classroom, five hundred years old, and made me sit at one of the desks. They're dark, heavy oak, thickly covered with boys' initials scratched into the wood with pocket knives. Five hundred years' worth of boys' initials is something to see.

We went into the chapel where the senior boys worship, there's a roll book hanging from the aisle pew of each row so that every boy's presence can be checked off by a monitor. We read the names in one – 'Harris Major. Harris Minor. Harris Tertius' – Eton never does in English what it can do in Latin.

Along the hall outside the classrooms the high oak walls have names cut into them as thickly as the initials in the desks. PB told me when a boy graduates he pays a few shillings to the college to have his name carved in the wall. We saw Pitt's name and Shelley's (and PB showed me his own). You could spend a month crawling up and down the walls looking for names.

Heart-rending plaques to Eton's war dead. One family lost eight men in World War I, seven of them in their twenties. The Grenfells (Joyce Grenfell's husband's family) lost grandfather, father and one son – and six men in the Boer War a dozen years earlier.

We went outside and saw the playing fields where all those wars were supposedly won. Boys were playing cricket, a few strolled by swinging tennis rackets. On Saturdays the boys are allowed to wear ordinary sports clothes but we saw several in the Eton uniform : black tail coat, white shirt, striped trousers. PB says they don't wear the top hat any more except on state occasions. (Those top hats kept the boys out of trouble. If an Eton boy tried to sneak into an off-limits pub or movie, the manager could spot that top hat from anywhere in the house and throw him out.)

The faces of the boys are unbelievably clean and chiseled and beautiful. And the tail coats – which must have looked outlandish in the 1940's and 50's – look marvelously appropriate with the long hair the boys wear now. What with the cameo faces, the long hair brushed to a gleam and the perfectly cut tails, they looked like improbable Edwardian princes.

We drove back to London at four; PB wanted to take me through Marlborough House and it closes at five and we had to stop off at his flat first to get his letter. The letter opens extra doors at Marlborough House the way the Eton tie did at Eton. It's on Marlborough House stationery, it's dated 1948, it begins 'Dear Cousin Buckley' and it's signed 'George R.' (If you're an ignorant citizen of the classless American republic, the R is for Rex. For George R read George VI.) I didn't read the letter, I think it invites him to show visitors through the house whenever he likes.

We drove to Marlborough House but couldn't go through it, the guard explained the house is closed for cleaning. The

Royal Chapel is open, and PB told me to go to services there one Sunday. He said it's never crowded or touristy since few people know it's open to the public. Queen Mary was married there, so I'm going, out of affection for her and Pope-Hennessy.

LATER

Laura Davidson just phoned from Oxford. She wrote me a fan letter telling me her husband, a Swarthmore professor, was working at Balliol for a year and that they and their fifteen-year-old son were fans of the book and wanted me to come to Oxford. I wrote back and told her when I was coming to London and she actually rescheduled a Paris vacation just so she'd be in Oxford when I came. When I picked up the phone just now and said hello, she said:

'Hi, it's Laura Davidson, how are you, when are you coming to Oxford? My son is dying of suspense.'

We settled on next Friday. She said there are trains almost every hour, call and let her know which one I'm on and she'll meet it. She'll carry the book so I'll know her.

I'm paranoid enough about traveling when I'm home and healthy, and the prospect of strange railroad stations and train trips over here kind of wears me out. But Oxford I have to see. There's one suite of freshman's rooms at Trinity College which John Donne, John Henry Newman and Arthur Quiller-Couch all lived in, in various long-gone eras. Whatever I know about writing English those three men taught me, and before I die I want to stand in their freshman's rooms and call their names blessed.

Q (Quiller-Couch) was all by himself my college education. I went down to the public library one day when I was seventeen looking for books on the art of writing, and found five books of lectures which Q had delivered to his students of writing at Cambridge.

'Just what I need!' I congratulated myself. I hurried home with the first volume and started reading and got to page 3 and hit a snag:

Q was lecturing to young men educated at Eton and Harrow. He therefore assumed that his students – including me –had read *Paradise Lost* as a matter of course and would understand his analysis of the 'Invocation to Light' in Book 9. So I said, 'Wait here,' and went down to the library and got *Paradise Lost* and took it home and started reading it and got to page 3, when I hit a snag :

Milton assumed I'd read the Christian version of Isaiah and the New Testament and had learned all about Lucifer and the War in Heaven, and since I'd been reared in Judaism I hadn't. So I said, 'Wait here,' and borrowed a Christian Bible and read about Lucifer and so forth, and then went back to Milton and read *Paradise Lost*, and then finally got back to Q, page 3. On page 4 or 5, I discovered that the point of the sentence at the top of the page was in Latin and the long quotation at the bottom of the page was in Greek. So I advertised in the *Saturday Review* for somebody to teach me Latin and Greek, and went back to Q meanwhile, and discovered he assumed I not only knew all the plays of Shakespeare, and Boswell's *Johnson*, but also the Second Book of Esdras, which is not in the Old Testament and not in the New Testament, it's in the Apocrypha, which is a set of books nobody had ever thought to tell me existed.

So what with one thing and another and an average of three 'Wait here's' a week, it took me eleven years to get through Q's five books of lectures.

Q also introduced me to John Henry Newman, who taught at Oriel, Oxford, and when I finish with Trinity I'm going over to Oriel and sit in John Henry's chapel and tell him I still don't know what he was talking about most of the time but I've got whole pages of the *Apologia* by heart, and I own a first edition of *The Idea of a University*.

PB is right, the Royal Chapel at Marlborough is not at all touristy and few people know it's open to the public. If it is.

I dressed very carefully and went down there this morning. Only a handful of people attended the service. All of them obviously worship there every Sunday, all of them obviously know each other and all of them spent most of the service trying to figure out who I was. From the whispers and sidelong glances you could reconstruct the dialogue:

'My dear, don't look now ...'

'... back there on the end pew, a few rows behind ...'

Bzz-bzz-bzz.

One angular, elderly lady got out her spectacles just to have a good long squint at me. Then she turned to the wispy friend sitting next to her and shook her head 'No!' firmly. The wispy lady refused to be daunted. She kept staring at me with the tentative half-smile you use when you know the face but just can't place it. I made the mistake of smiling back, and from then on neither of them took their eyes off me.

I was also the only shoulder bag in the house, if I have to add that.

At the end of the service I was the first one up the aisle and out of there.

Had to come back up here for lunch, NOTHING is open here on Sunday, you could starve.

AFTERNOON

I'm lying under a tree in St. James's Park. There are three downtown parks adjoining each other – St. James's and Green, both small, and the big one, Hyde Park.

All the parks here are very serene, very gentle. Young couples go by, arm in arm, quietly, no transistor radios or guitars in hand. Families picnic on the lawn sedately. Dogs go by on leashes, equally sedate, looking neither to the right nor to the left. There was one exception : a woman came by with a small gray poodle on a leash, I said hello to the poodle and he veered toward me, always-glad-to-meet-a-friend, but the woman yanked him back.

'Please don't do that!' she said to me sharply. 'I'm trying to teach him good manners.'

I thought, 'A pity he can't do the same for you,' and had a sudden vision of Dog Hill on a Sunday afternoon and wondered how everybody was.

We had a picnic there one night – Dick, who lives in my building and owns an English sheep dog, and my friend Nikki and I. I had some cold turkey for sandwiches and I deviled some eggs, and Dick made a thermos of bloody marys and we went over to the hill with Chester-the-Sheep-Dog. Nikki came up from her office and met us there. You have to be crazy to picnic on Dog Hill, but Dick and I thought we'd try it. We didn't get there till six-thirty, most of the dogs had gone home.

Dog Hill is a broad, sloping hill in Central Park, and the largest canine Social Hall in the world. On a weekend afternoon you'll see forty or fifty dogs up there, charging around off leash meeting friends. (You don't take a dog to Dog Hill unless he's a friend to the world but I never met a New York dog who wasn't.) On a good day you'll see everything from Afghans and Norwegian elkhounds to Shih-tzus and Lhasa Apsos, not to mention all the standard brands. The dog owners sit on the grass or stand around like parents at a children's party, keeping an eye out for sudden spats over whose stick it is or whose ball it is.

'George, if you can't play nicely we're going home!'

'Mabel, get off him! I don't wanna hear about it, just get off him!'

You do not stretch out on the grass to sunbathe because if a couple of great Danes and a collie are having a race and you're lying in their path they're not going to detour for you.

Dick and Nikki and I settled at the top of the hill and Dick poured out the bloody marys in paper cups. A few dogs were playing halfway down the hill, and normally Chester-the-Sheep-Dog would have joined them. But he'd smelled the picnic basket all the way to the park so he just loped down the hill and sniffed everybody and then came back up, figuring he'd hang around us till dinner time.

I understood this, so when I got out the sandwiches I gave Chester a sliver of turkey out of mine. That was all it took. In five seconds, there was a semicircle of dogs in front of me : every dog left on the hill had come to the picnic.

There were two basset-hound brothers named Sam and Sid, Romulus, who is a great Dane, a beagle I didn't know and a very timid German shepherd pup named Helga – all standing stock still, eyes glued to me and my turkey sandwich. The beagle was drooling.

I had an extra sandwich in reserve so I sacrificed the one I'd started on and gave each dog in turn a sliver of turkey. (Helga was very nervous, she was anxious to step up for her piece of turkey but how did she know I wouldn't bite her?)

Chester-the-Sheep-Dog figured there was too much competition, so he left and trotted back to visit Nikki's sandwich. And just as I was feeding the rest of the dogs the last of the turkey, Nikki set up a great to-do because Chester had taken a sip of her bloody mary. Dick called, 'Chester! Sit!' And Chester, wanting to show how well-trained he was, sat on Nikki's deviled egg. Whereupon Nikki took a fit. (She's young and pretty and she went to the London School of Economics for a year, but she's a cat lover.) I turned and called Chester, hoping to lure him away from her – and the instant my back was turned, the beagle (Morton, I think his name was) seized the untouched reserve sandwich and made off down the hill with it.

His mother came up to apologize and thank me; she said he only eats chicken and now she wouldn't have to cook for him when they got home.

We walked back down through the park to the Seventy-second Street entrance, past a baseball game and an impromptu marimba band fighting a rock concert that penetrated clear up from Fifty-ninth Street.

Lying in peaceful St. James's, I realize how much a city's parks reflect the character of its people. The parks here are tranquil, quiet, a bit reserved, and I love them. But on a long-term basis I would sorely miss the noisy exuberance of Central Park.

9 P.M.

The Colonel phoned up, he's back. He said, What part of our glorious countryside did I want to see most? I told him I was going to Oxford next Friday and I'd be very grateful if he wanted to drive me there.

'Well, now!' he boomed. 'We can do much better than that, my dear! If you're free on Thursday, we can drive through the Cotswolds and be in Stratford-on-Avon in time for dinner and the theatre, and drive on to meet your friends in Oxford on Friday.'

I was wildly excited, which surprised me. I'm not terribly attracted to birthplaces, to me Shakespeare was born in the Globe Theatre. But when he said he was taking me to Stratford-on-Avon I shouted in my excitement, you can't help it.

Asked if he knew a shop where I could buy a cheap overnight bag and he said:

'Nonsense, I'll send a nice BOAC bag round to you.'

I tell you it's insidious being an ersatz Duchess, people rushing to give you what you want before you've had time to want it. If I kept this up for more than a month it would ruin my moral fiber.

I'd left my number with Leo Mark's answering service and he called back this morning. He has a beautiful Oxford baritone. (Or Cambridge, I don't know the difference.) He and his wife will pick me up for dinner tomorrow night at seven.

Dinner and *Midsummer Night* with the Grenfells tonight, so this morning I took my cocktail dress downstairs and said to the young desk clerk :

'Can I have this pressed before five this evening?'

'D'you want it cleaned or laundered?' he asked.

'No, just pressed,' I said.

He stared at me blankly.

'Do you want it sent to the Cleaner's?' he repeated, emphasizing each word as carefully as if I were Russian or deaf, 'or do you want it sent to the Laundry?'

'I don't want it cleaned *or* washed,' I said, enunciating as carefully as if *he* were Russian or deaf, 'I just want it *pressed*. It's *wrinkled*.'

This seemed to stun him. He stared at me a moment. Then he pulled himself together, mumbled, ''Scuse me,' and went off to consult the Office. In a minute he was back.

'If you'll go up to Room 315 and speak to the house-keeper,' he said, 'p'raps she can help you.'

I went up and knocked on the door of Room 315 and explained my problem to the motherly-looking housekeeper. She nodded understandingly and said, 'Come this way, dear,' and led me down to the end of the hall and opened the door to a little dungeon with an ironing board and an ancient monster iron in one corner.

'You can press it right here, dear,' she said. 'Mind the iron, the cord's a bit frayed.'

I was a bit frayed myself by this time. The dress is silk, the iron was unfamiliar and didn't look friendly. I took the dress down to the desk and told the clerk to send it to the Cleaner's, he was very relieved. This is what comes of being allergic to chemical fabrics in a drip-dry world.

I got lost trying to find the Waldorf on foot, overshot it by two blocks, ran back and tore into the lobby ten minutes late – and Joyce Grenfell must have been watching the door, she came out to meet me looking exactly as she looks on the screen.

She led the way into the dining room and introduced me to her husband – 'RegGEE!' she mostly calls him – and their Australian friends, Sir Charles and Lady Fitts, he's a famous doctor. I sat down, suddenly shaken by the fact that these four distinguished people had wanted to meet *me*. I tell you, life is extraordinary. A few years ago I couldn't write anything or sell anything, I'd passed the age where you know all the returns are in, I'd had my chance and done my best and failed. And how was I to know the miracle waiting to happen round the corner in late middle age? *84, Charing Cross Road* was no best seller, you understand; it didn't make me rich or famous. It just got me hundreds of letters and phone calls from people I never knew existed; it got me wonderful reviews; it restored a self-confidence and self-esteem I'd lost somewhere along the way, God knows how many years ago. It brought me to England. It changed my life.

The Grenfells had got house seats for themselves and the Australians, and when Joyce read I was in town she invited me along – even though it meant Reggie had to give up his house seat to me and go sit in the balcony, I was horrified.

It's an experience walking down a theatre aisle with a famous theatre personality. Every eye in the audience was on her, and when we took our seats you could feel necks craning all over the house.

Peter Brook's production initially a shock, half play, half noisy circus. Mrs. G. was immediately entranced; I kept worrying about whether Puck was going to fall off his stilts or drop the plates he was juggling. Halfway through the second act I was suddenly moved, and I thought, 'I resent it but I love it.' Stimulates you to death, seeing Shakespeare explode all over a stage like that.

They drove me home after saying goodbye to the Australians. Joyce drove because it's a new car and Reggie wanted her to get the feel of it.

She had a hell of a time in Bloomsbury. The one-way streets here set drivers crazy, you have to go five blocks out of your way to find a street going in the right direction. And she was NOT going to drop me across Shaftesbury Avenue on the wrong corner of Great Russell Street, she would NOT drop me round the corner on Bloomsbury Street, the hotel entrance was on Great Russell and she was By God going to drop me in front of the door. And after zigzagging north and south for half an hour she triumphantly did it and accepted my congratulations graciously.

She said they're 'going on holiday' but will be back on July 13 for her church dialogue. She has a monthly church dialogue with a minister – on The Nature of Love and The Nature of Beauty and so forth – at a noon service at St. Mary LeBeau's Church in Cheapside. She said Why don't I come to the July 13 dialogue and then come to dinner that night and they'll drive me around to see the sights. I told her I wasn't certain I'd still be here on the thirteenth, though I'm hoping to last till the fifteenth.

During the second act, that cold caught up with me. I started to cough and nearly strangled trying to muffle it. I leaned over and whispered to Joyce apologetically :

'I've been fighting a cold all weekend.'

She thought about this a moment and then leaned over and whispered back :

'Oh, have it.'

So I'm having it. Sitting up in bed hacking and snuffling and even that doesn't depress me. I seem to be living in a state of deep hypnosis, every time I mail a postcard home I could use Euphoria for a return address.

I'm in the dining room having my fourth or fifth cup of coffee, feeling the way you feel the first morning of a full-blown cold. I was going to call Leo Marks and cancel dinner but if I stay in the hotel all day I'll want to get out of it to-night so I'll keep the date and try not to cough in their faces.

The dining room's emptying out now; between eight and nine every morning it's jammed and the waiters are frantic. The room rate here includes 'Full English Breakfast' and we all eat everything : fruit juice or cereal, bacon and eggs, toast and marmalade, tea or coffee (and the girl who brings the coffee pot asks : 'Black or white?').

The breakfast regulars always include British Willie Lomans up from the country on business and a sprinkling of middle-aged women from all over 'the U.K.' traveling alone. (They never say 'Great Britain,' it's 'the U.K.' – United Kingdom.) Several pale, pointy-nosed professors are stowing away enough fuel to see them through the day at the British museum, they all look as if they lunch on yogurt.

This morning, a long table of Scots matrons here for a con-ference accompanied by a scrubbed young vicar. Ladies all complained they didn't sleep a *wink* for the noise, the motor-cars go by in the street just-all-NIGHT. Quietest place I ever slept in. They should try tucking up over Second Avenue, where the trucks start rolling at 3 A.M.

Lots of Russian and Czech tourist families here, with blond, well-behaved children. Several parties of German tourists, middle-aged to make it worse. (The young ones you don't mind; they-didn't-do-it.) The tourist parties all eat with one eye on the clock, they've all signed up for some bus tour and the buses leave the hotel at nine sharp. At two minutes to nine there's a heavy Russian-Czech-German bustle and a ponderous exodus to the lobby – where the Czechs gesticulate wildly at signs they can't read and the German tour leader bawls, '*Achtung!*' and, '*Halte!*' to get everybody lined up. The Russians just stolidly find the bus and get on it.

The only Americans here besides me turned up at breakfast this morning for the first time : three California college girls, blond, tanned, radiantly healthy, conferring anxiously on whether Full English Breakfast meant you could order everything, it's all free with the room? I asked the waitress for more coffee and when they heard my American accent one of them came over to my table to ask about what you can order and Are you supposed to tip. I said No, the management adds 12 per cent to your bill for tips. Alvaro was scandalized when I tried to tip him the first day. No, No! he said, It is all cared for!

Will now retire to my room with last weekend's newspapers and their fiendish crossword puzzles and spend the morning 'enjoying poor health,' as my mother used to say.

Crime Note

From Saturday's evening paper :

£50 FINE FOR TEACHER
WHO ASSAULTED GIRL
AT WIMBLEDON

A 54-year-old teacher of statistics at London University . . . appeared in court today charged with insulting behavior at Wimbledon tennis championships.

He was fined £50 after admitting indecent assault in the standing area of No. 1 Court.

Temporary Det. Con. Patrick Doyle told Wimbledon magistrates that [the defandant] put an arm around an 18-year-old girl and held her breasts.

[The defendant], who is married, said :

'I suffered a temporary lapse of commonsense.

'It is ridiculous that a man in my position should do such a thing.'

A Wimbledon umpire . . . aged 66, was also accused of insulting behavior at Wimbledon. Altogether 10 men appeared, charged with insulting behavior.

The sixty-six-year-old umpire was extra lucky, they put his picture in the paper.

Here's a help-wanted ad for you :

BUCKINGHAM PALACE. Vacancy in the central
wash-up of the main kitchen, for female applicants
only. Non-residential. . . . Apply in writing to Mas-
ter of the Household, Buckingham Palace, London
SW 1

Wouldn't you like to take that job for one day, just to
listen to the gossip?

11 P.M.

Leo Marks phoned up from the lobby at seven, I went
down to meet them in my silk-dress-and-coat, red nose and
watery eyes, and Leo, who is dark-haired and good-looking,
said :

'How d'you do, we're very glad you could come, go back
upstairs and get a coat, it's chilly and it's raining.'

I came up and got my old blue coat, went down and told
him :

'You've made me ruin the effect of my whole costume.'

And Ena – his wife, very small and blond – said earnestly :

'You can take the coat off when we get to the restaurant,
we're dining at a hotel, you can take it off in the lobby !' and
peered at me anxiously to see if that was all right.

She ought to look delicate but doesn't, you get a sense of
wiry strength. She might be a small blond athlete but she's
a portrait painter. She paints under her own name, Ena
Gaussen. Leo told me she's done portraits for Hayley Mills
and Pamela Brown and won all sorts of citations; she
doesn't look old enough.

They took me to the Stafford, a very old, gracious hotel
rather like the Plaza. I had a couple of martinis to clear
the sinuses and discovered Leo is a gin drinker. He's also a
TV and film writer and we found we'd worked for the same

TV producer – in different seasons and on different continents – and we talked shop. Ena didn't mind, she thinks we're both terribly witty.

He calls her 'little thing.'

'Little thing, you want the lobster again?'

He asked me if I knew of the pianist Eileen Joyce and told me : 'She's just been made a Dame of the British Empire and she wants the little thing to paint her in her Dame's robes.'

When it was too late to go see it, Ena told me one of Leo's films was playing around the corner; I was very impressed. I've always believed film writing is the most difficult form a writer can work in.

'Tell me,' said Leo. 'You've written a beautiful book. Why haven't we heard of you before? What was wrong with your earlier work? Too good or not good enough?'

'Not good enough,' I said. And he nodded and went on to something else, and I think that's when we became soul mates.

It was a marvelous evening. I'd love to see them again but I haven't the nerve to call and suggest it. Being a visiting fireman has its own courtesy rules.

cough-cough-cough-cough-cough.

Being a celebrity means you're paged to the phone three times during breakfast, and the first time you come back to the table your eggs are cold, the second time you come back your eggs are GONE and the third time you carry a fresh plate of eggs out to the lobby phone booth with you.

Joyce Grenfell phoned to ask how my cough was and to say Do-be-here-on-the-thirteenth. I told her I mean to. The hotel switchboard operator recognized her voice and didn't put the call through to the booth, I took it at the desk, and the switchboard operator and cashier both like to collapse when I held the receiver out so they could hear her call, 'RegGEEE!' when she wanted to ask him something.

Nora phoned and heard my croak and said Why didn't I come out to North London and let her nurse me? That's all she needs; she's working at a full-time job since Frank died.

The Colonel phoned to say the BOAC bag 'will be sent round this A.M.' and he'll pick me up at ten tomorrow morning for the trip to Stratford-and-Oxford.

After breakfast I went across the street for Kleenex and cough drops. There's a string of small stores opposite the hotel on Great Russell Street: a stationery store, a Unisex Beauty Shop, a Cinema Bookshop and an Indian food store that carries health-food items. There's also a large YWCA Women's Residence and a curb-side fruit stand. I stopped at the fruit stand for some peaches, and while I was waiting for change I noticed a bulletin board in a glass case outside the stationery store. Got my change and went over to read the bulletin board. At first glance the notices seem to be Items-for-Sale and Situations-Wanted ads, but you don't have to read very far to discover your mistake. To the pure in heart, however, all bulletin boards are pure, viz.: (This is the entire bulletin-board list.)

Hot Pants for sale. Phone ....

Ex-actress will give lessons. French or anything. Phone ....

Male model. All services. TV, photog, rubber, leather. Corrective training. Phone ....

Model seeks unusual positions. Miss Coucher. Phone ....

New lovely blonde doll for sale. Walks, talks. Phone ....

Tom Tamer gives lessons in the most strict deportment. Phone ....

French girl. Ex-governess, many positions. Seeks new pupils. Both sexes. Phone ....

Three rucksacks wanted. Good condition. Reasonable. Contact YWCA, Great Russell St.

7 P.M.

Ena blew in at five-thirty with a brown paper bag full of lemons, honey and lime juice for my cough. She said she had an urge all morning to call me and hang on the phone but felt shy about it; I said we're both too inhibited. She wanted me to have dinner with them tomorrow night. I told her I'd be in Stratford but would be back Friday, and her face fell.

'We go down to the country on Friday and we won't be back until the tenth !' she said.

'Never mind,' I said. 'I have every intention of lasting till the fifteenth.'

She looked distressed.

'You can't go home that soon ! We've only just met you !'

she said. 'Look, when you run out of money why don't you go down and stay at our place in the country? We shan't be using it at all after the tenth, you could stay there all summer – if you don't mind our coming down weekends?' peering at me anxiously. People unhinge me.

She just left to meet Leo at his mother's.

The BOAC bag arrived, and I phoned the Colonel and thanked him. He advised me to eat a lot :

'You must always feed a cold. If you don't give the germs food to eat they'll feed on you.'

Will now go down to the dining room and feed the germs.

LATER

I ordered 'Chicken Maryland,' which turned out to be a slice of chicken, breaded and fried flat like a veal cutlet, accompanied by a strip of bacon and a fat sausage. Dessert was 'Coupe Jamaica,' I didn't order it but the couple at the next table did : a long, narrow cookie sticking out of a ball of vanilla ice cream that rested on a slice of canned pineapple. It would probably confuse Jamaica as much as the chicken would confuse Maryland. But somebody once told me there's a restaurant in Paris that lists on the menu 'Pommes à la French Fries.'

I'm writing this in bed, in a luxurious motel room : wall-to-wall carpet, easy chair, TV set, dressing table and a beautiful adjoining bath in mauve tile, life at the Kenilworth was never like this.

I tell you my Colonel has got to be the world's kindest, most considerate man. We left London in the usual gray weather, it gets to you after a while; I told him I was beginning to crave sunshine the way a thirsty man craves water. We drove into the Cotswolds and about mid-morning the weather cleared and the sun came out briefly. The minute it did, he pulled over to the side of the road, got a deck chair out of the trunk and set it up on a stretch of grass for me so I could lie in the sun the little while it lasted. He told me his wife died of cancer 'after two years of hell'; he must have been marvelous through it.

We passed Stoke Poges and he told me that's where Gray's country churchyard is. Gray's 'Elegy' was my mother's favorite poem, I'd like to have seen the churchyard but we didn't have time for the detour.

As we drove, he told me a long-winded story about a widow he knows who fell in love with a man and was invited to his villa in Italy, and when she got there she found she had no room of her own, the man actually meant her to share his BEDroom, d'ye see, and Well-I-mean-to-say, said the Colonel, she wasn't aTALL that sort, and it was a shock to find the Bounder wanted only One Thing. I wondered why he told me the story since he didn't figure in it – and then it dawned on me that this was his tactful way of assuring me he didn't expect me to share his bedroom in Stratford. It had never occurred to me; he's much too strait-laced and old-school, it would have been out of character.

He told me he retired from publishing to nurse his wife, and after she died he took the job at Heathrow for the fun of it.

'If I see a man and his wife and grown daughters standing together looking a bit out of sorts, I walk up to the man and say : "Sir, which of these ladies is your wife?" And he beams! And she beams!' And the Colonel roars with laughter.

'If I see a middle-aged couple looking a bit down, you know, I walk up to them and ask : "Are you folks on your honeymoon?" and you ought to see their faces! They know I'm joshing – some of 'em do – but still, y'know, they can't help being pleased.

'If I see a child crying – some of them get very tired and upset at a big airport, they're hungry, they want to be at home – and when I see one crying I walk up and ask the parents if they know where I can find a nice little girl because mine is grown up. And then I discover the little girl who's crying and I say she's exactly the sort of little girl I've been looking for, and I ask if she'd consider being my little girl.' And he ends each story with that booming laugh of pure pleasure.

The Cotswolds are just what I always thought they'd be : stretches of green countryside pocketed with English villages that seem not to have changed since the time of Elizabeth I. We had lunch at a pub near a country church where, said the Colonel, 'Hampden started the Revolution.' Didn't have the nerve to tell him I don't know who Hampden was.

Stratford is beyond Oxford, we backtrack tomorrow. We passed Oxford road signs and I told him about Great Tew. Years ago, somebody sent me a postcard – a photograph of five thatched cottages falling down a hillside – and wrote on the back :

This is Great Tew. You can't find it on the map, you have to get lost on the way to Oxford.

The photo was so idealized a view of rural England I didn't believe the village really existed. I used to stare at that postcard by the hour. Kept it for years, stuck in my Oxford English Verse.

'Well!' said the Colonel, inspired by the challenge. 'We shall just have to find Great Tew and see if it's still the same.'

He wove in and out through the Cotswolds and finally we came to signs pointing to Tew and Little Tew and rounded a curve and there was Great Tew, looking exactly as it had looked on my postcard: five ancient stone houses with thatched roofs, still falling down the hillside. The Colonel said they date back to Henry VIII. Five hundred years later they're still lived in: there were white curtains and flower boxes at the windows, and every front lawn had a rose garden.

He parked the car – the only car in sight – and we got out. Down the road from the cottages was the village's only other building, a one-room General Store and Post Office. We went in. There was no one in there but the woman who runs it, and we hadn't seen a soul outside.

The Colonel bought ice cream, I asked for a glass of milk and was handed a quart bottle and a straw. The Colonel told the proprietress that I had come 'all the way from New York' and had 'particularly asked to see Great Tew.' While they talked I was clutching the quart bottle, entirely pre-occupied with trying to get at least half a pint of it inside me so as not hurt her feelings. When I'd drunk that much I looked around for an inobtrusive place to park the bottle, and discovered that the store had suddenly filled up with people – men in country caps and women in print dresses. I moved out of their way and they all stepped up to the counter and bought cigarettes and newspapers. A few children came in and were promptly shooed out by the proprietress.

The Colonel finished his ice cream, took my milk bottle off my hands and disposed of a pint and a half of milk as if it were a glass of water, and we left.

'Well!' he said as we walked back to the car. 'We've given them something to talk about for a month! Did you notice how the entire village came in to see the people from Outer Space? As soon as they saw my car with the London plates they came running. Did you see how she shooed the kids out? That was to make room for all the grownups. They won't see travelers here from one year's end to the next. And from New York? Not in a lifetime!'

And we were a few hours from London by car.

Everybody I ever knew who went to Stratford had warned me that it was a commercial tourist trap, so I was prepared for it. The first thing we saw as we drove in was a huge billboard advertising the JUDITH SHAKESPEARE WIMPY HAMBURGER BAR, the Colonel was purple with fury. It doesn't matter in the least. You find Shakespeare's house and pay your fee to enter – and just to walk up the stairs gripping the huge railing, just to walk into the bedroom and touch the walls, and then come back down and stand in the kitchen that saw him in and out every day of his growing up has to melt the bones of anyone born speaking English.

We saw *Much Ado* at the shiny modern theatre, very conventional, not very well acted. The Colonel slept through most of it and I didn't blame him.

Will now go climb into that mauve bathtub, we leave for Oxford early in the morning and I mean to get the most out of this posh palace first.

I saw Trinity College and walked the Yard John Donne walked; I saw Oriel and sat in John Henry's chapel. And what I went through to see them, you purely will not credit. I think I finally had a temper tantrum. I hope I did.

We reached Oxford a little before noon and found the Davidson's house on a typical tree-shaded, college-town street. Laura was there waiting for us. She said the Professor was working and son David was in school counting the hours till he could join us for tea.

She has a throaty voice and a lovely, odd accent; she was born in Vienna and grew up in England. She and her husband were both refugee children from Hitler's Germany.

She was vastly amused by the Colonel, she called him 'the Commahnder' and said he reminded her of Winnie the Pooh. My problem was that by this time the Colonel and I had already had thirty straight hours of Togetherness and I'm not equipped for it, not even with the best friend I have on earth, which he isn't. Over lunch in a campus pub, he announced (à propos of nothing, I think he was just carried away by Oxford):

'The British Empire will be brought back by popular demand! An Egyptian said to me recently: "Why do you English sit modestly at home when you're needed all over the world?"'

For some reason this aggravated me and I said something rude, and we had at it for a couple of minutes till Laura tactfully inserted herself between us like a housemother, and restored harmony.

After lunch, my troubles started. I said Could we please go see Trinity and Oriel Colleges? and Laura said First we must visit the Bodleian Reading Room, it was a magnificent Wren building and her husband was working there and wanted to meet me. We went there and I met the Professor and saw the Reading Room, vaulted ceiling, towering shelves and staircases, all spectacular.

We came out, and I said Now could we go see Trinity

and Oriel? and Laura said Did I know the Bodleian library stacks ran for a mile under the pavements? and showed me which pavements. And the Colonel said he had studied one summer at Wadham College and I must see Wadham Yard. And he and Laura agreed they must take me down the main street to Blackwell's Bookshop, very famous bookshop and they both knew how interested I was in bookshops. (I despair of ever getting it through anybody's head I am not interested in bookshops, I am interested in what's written in the books. I don't browse in bookshops, I browse in libraries, where you can take a book home and read it, and if you like it you go to a bookshop and buy it.)

So, on the one shining day of my life when I was actually in Oxford, I'm dragged down the main street, I'm having every monument and every church pointed out to me, they're all by Wren (everything's by Wren), I'm hauled through Blackwell's Bookshop table by table and shelf by shelf, and the next thing I know I'm walking around the Yard of some place called Wadham, for God's sake. And it's getting later and later, any minute we'll be off to Laura's house to meet her son for tea and after tea the Colonel and I will be leaving for London.

So I had a tantrum.

I stood in the middle of Wadham Yard and hollered: 'WHEN ARE WE GONNA SEE SOMETHING *I* WANNA SEE?'

Laura hurried over to me and got very kindly and understanding (she used to be a Social Worker) and said:

'The Commahnder's loving it. Wadham is his only link with Oxford.'

And I replied reasonably: 'HE LIVES OVER HERE, HE CAN SEE IT ANY DAMN DAY HE WANTS TO!'

And she said Sh-sh, and the Colonel strode over and said What is it? What's the matter? And they both thought it over and decided I was right, Now what was it I specially wanted to see? And Laura said Was I sure there was an Oriel College, she couldn't find it on her map, and the Colonel said Was I perhaps thinking of Trinity-Cambridge, Prince Charles had gone to Trinity-Cambridge.

And I said carefully No, I was thinking of John Henry Newman, who taught Anglican theology at Oriel College and died a Catholic cardinal and was a little cracked in many ways but who wrote English like few men on God's green earth ever wrote English, one of the few being John Donne, and they both went to Trinity-Oxford, so could I please see Trinity and Oriel.

We came out of Wadham Yard and stood on a corner and Laura studied her map again and sure enough, there was an Oriel College. We went there and I sat in the chapel by myself and communed with John Henry. (Outside, I learned later, the Colonel was telling Laura I was 'a crazy, mixed-up kid.')

We went to Trinity and I walked around the Yard. And that was all. Tourists are not allowed inside the college buildings.

Unless you're interested chiefly in the architecture, visiting Oxford is very frustrating. All that is open to tourists at any college is the Yard outside it and the chapel just inside the front door. Everything else is off limits. So I'll never see those freshman's rooms and I'll never know whether there is still 'much snap-dragon' growing outside the window, as there was in Newman's day. And I'll never see the rooms Milton wrote in or the rooms Q taught in at Cambridge because Cambridge has the same restrictions.

We got back to Laura's house – five minutes before fifteen-year-old David came home panting and breathless, he'd run all the way just to meet me, I've never been so flattered.

The Colonel had a cup of tea and then marched off to a bedroom and took a nap and Laura and David and I sat in the kitchen and swapped stories about Philadelphia, where their home is and where I grew up. They go back in September.

Over tea, Laura got very guilt-ridden about my day and begged me to sneak back up on a train one day and do Oxford by myself. ('Don't even let us know you're here if you don't want to,' she said, and David said, 'Why can't she let us know she's here?') I told her I'd seen what I most wanted to see – and within the limits of what was possible, it was true.

Driving back to London we passed a village called Thame – pronounced as spelled, like 'same' with a lisp – and the Colonel told me why the Thames is pronounced Temmes. Seems the first Hanover king had a thick German accent and couldn't pronounce *th*. He called the river 'te Temmes' and since the-king-is-always-right everybody else had to call it the Temmes and it's been the Temmes ever since.

He told me about all the widows who depend on him for advice, they all seem to have 'lashings of money' and children who adore him.

We got home at nine. I'll be grateful to him all my life for the trip, but it was a lot of togetherness. I holed up in the bar to write this; the Lounge is more comfortable and also free but anybody who talked to me tonight would've got bit.

Flock of messages for me at the desk. Marc Connelly phoned, the London *Reader's Digest* phoned, Nikki's Barbara phoned and a woman I never heard of phoned. The desk clerk was very impressed by all the messages. So was I.

I just called Marc Connelly. He was a reigning play-wright when I was a child and my parents were rabid theatregoers. They should have lived to see the fan letter he wrote me. It came just before Christmas and I almost threw it away without opening it. His name is on some way-out charity I don't care for, and I thought the letter was another appeal. Not till my hand was hovering over the wastebasket did it occur to me that the envelope was very thin for a charity appeal. So I opened it.

Dear Miss Hanff :

What with all those other letters closing in on you (How many grateful people have written up to now – one million? two million?) I don't expect you'll get around to reading this for a year or more.

Anyway, sooner or later you'll find it's just like all the others : telling you that '84, Charing Cross Road' is tender and funny and incandescent and beautiful and makes the reader rejoice to be living in the same century with you.

Genuflections,

Marc Connelly

And I almost threw it away without opening it.

I met him a few months later, and he told me he'd be in London in July, at his club, and he'd take me to see what a gentleman's club looks like.

He'll pick me up tomorrow at one for lunch.

Can't call Nikki's Barbara or the *Reader's Digest* till Monday, both offices are closed Saturdays. Nikki – the friend whose deviled egg Chester-the-Sheep-Dog sat on at our Central Park picnic – works for a news magazine in New York. Barbara works for the same news magazine in London. The two girls have never met but they talk to each other every day over the teletype so they're good friends. Nikki made us promise to meet while I'm here.

I can definitely make it till the fifteenth, dinner invitations coming in nicely. I just phoned that woman I never heard of who called while I was away. She said she and her husband are fans of the book and want me to come to dinner to see their part of London. I'm going there Tuesday.

Every breathing tourist who has breakfast in this hotel has seen a piece of royalty but me. (How I know is, whoever is breakfasting alone at the next table strikes up a conversation with you, usually beginning with, *Might* I trouble you for the marmalade?') Either they saw the Family leave for Windsor, or they were getting on the elevator at Harrods just as the Queen Mother was getting off it, or they saw Princess Anne wave as she entered the hospital, or they just-by-good-chance happened to be passing by this boys' school as seven-year-old Prince Edward was coming out with the other boys. So this morning I'm going down to Buckingham Palace and try my luck.

10 P.M.

Went down to Buckingham Palace, walked up and down along the spiked iron fence for a while but all I saw was one more anachronism : a seventeenth-century carriage drawn by white horses, driven through the gates by a fancy-dress coachman, and inside the carriage a pair of cold-eyed diplomats in top hats with cigarettes hanging out of their twentieth-century faces.

I find the treatment of royalty distinctly peculiar. The royal family lives in palaces heavily screened from prying eyes by fences, grounds, gates, guards, all designed to ensure the family absolute privacy. And every newspaper in London carried headlines announcing PRINCESS ANNE HAS OVARIAN CYST REMOVED. I mean you're a young girl reared in heavily guarded seclusion and every beer drinker in every pub knows the precise state of your ovaries.

Walked home by way of Lincoln's Inn Fields, a park this side of the Inns of Court facing a lovely row of houses on a street called King's Bench Walk. Sat on a bench and looked at the houses and listened to the conversations going by:

'. . . well, not uncouth, he looks like a Highland rabbi.'

'. . . but she wasn't getting anywhere out there so she packed it in and now she's home, looking . . .'

'They're all out to save their own neckties, you can bloody well bet on that!'

I'm in the bar again. I don't normally drink after dinner but in this hotel they think you're strange if you drink *before* dinner. So at 10 P.M. I'm having a martini. More or less.

The first night I came in here I said to the young bartender:

'A martini, please.'

He reached for a bottle of Martini & Rossi vermouth and poured a glass full of it before I could scream WAIT A MINUTE!

'Would you put the gin in first, please?' I asked.

'Oh!' he said. 'You want a *gin* martini.'

He got the gin bottle and a shaker, and I said:

'Would you put some ice in the shaker, please? I like it cold.'

'Right-o!' he said. He put an ice cube in the shaker, poured a jigger of gin on it, added half a cup of vermouth, stirred once, poured it out and handed it to me with a flourish. I paid him and shuffled over to a table telling myself sternly:

'Don't be like all those American tourists who can't adapt to another country's customs, just drink it.'

Nobody could drink it.

The next time I came in it was dinner time, the bar was empty and the bartender and I got chummy; he said Wasn't I the writer?? and told me his name was Bob. I said Did he mind if this time we used my recipe instead of his and he said Right-o, just tell him exactly what I wanted.

I said First could we start with four ice cubes in the shaker. He thought I was crazy but he put three cubes in (he was short on ice). He poured a jigger of gin in the shaker, and I said:

'Okay, now another jigger of gin.'

He stared at me, shook his head in disbelief and added a second jigger of gin.

'Okay, now one more,' I said.

'MORE gin?' he said, and I said :

'Yes, and lower your voice.'

He poured the third jigger, still shaking his head. He reached for the vermouth bottle, and I said :

'I'll pour that.'

I added a few drops of vermouth, stirred vigorously, let him pour it out for me and told him it was perfect.

Now he makes it by himself but he never can bring himself to add that third jigger of gin, he thinks he'll look up later and see me sprawled face down on a bar table sodden drunk.

Got very gloomy remembering the days before the Viet Nam War when I gloried in my country's history and July 4 meant something.

Marc Connelly picked me up at one. I wore the brown skirt and white blazer, and he said, 'Don't you look fine in your little yachting outfit,' and saluted. He said we'd have lunch at the Hilton because nothing else is open.

The Hilton has several dining rooms, he took me into the largest. It was crowded with sleek, well-groomed men and beautifully dressed women; nobody looked dowdy the way they do at the Kenilworth. And the strawberries were huge and the cream was thick and the rolls were hot and the butter was cold and the chicken livers were done to perfection.

But at the Kenilworth, nobody sends the eggs back. Nobody talks to the waiters with the casual rudeness that says, 'I am better than you are because I am richer.' And the waiters don't answer with that studied blend of contempt and servility, and none are obsequious – my God, Alvaro couldn't even pronounce it. And nobody at a Kenilworth breakfast table looks bitter or discontented, no men at the Kenilworth moodily drink their lunch, no women with hard-painted faces keep a sharp eye on their handbags.

You look at the faces in the Hilton dining room and first you want to smack them and then you just feel sorry for them, not a soul in the room looked happy.

After lunch Marc took me to his club on St. James's Street. The building looks narrow from the street; but you step through the doorway into an enormous drawing room with other large rooms beyond it, you climb a great curved staircase, the wall alongside lined with portraits of club presidents all looking like Peter Ustinov, and upstairs you find more spacious rooms – breakfast room, game rooms, reading rooms. We watched cricket for a while on color TV in one of the game rooms. At least, I watched it. Marc went to sleep. He's eighty, he's allowed.

I woke him at three to say I was leaving and he said

cheerfully, 'Now you know what I think of cricket!' and saw me to the door and told me to walk down Jermyn Street and look in the shop windows.

I did that, and then went over to Regent and was walking down Waterloo on my way to St. James's Park when who should I run into, standing on a corner on a little pedestal looking small and spruce, but Gentlemanly Johnny Burgoyne who lost the Battle of Saratoga to us rebels. I think he was supposed to link up with some other general's forces but there was a snafu and Burgoyne's entire army was captured. He'd be pleased to know he's the most appealing character in *The Devil's Disciple*, he was a playwright himself. He wrote a play and produced it in Boston, with his officers in the cast, when his troops occupied the city. Can't imagine what possessed the British to put up a statue to him, I suppose he won some battle somewhere but he lost the American Revolution almost singlehanded.

Wished him a happy Fourth.

When I got down to the Mall there was a band concert going on. In honor of the Fourth of July the band played 'Dixie' and 'The Battle Hymn of the Republic.' Well, why not? I don't know who Hampden was, why should they know July Fourth doesn't commemorate the Civil War?

Sunned myself in St. James's Park for a while but the band concert went on and on and I wasn't in the mood so I thought I'd walk up to Lincoln's Inn Fields instead. I couldn't get back up the broad marble steps, they were jammed with concert listeners, so I walked along the Mall looking for another exit. I came to a small flight of steps, maneuvered my way around the people sitting on them and came up into Carlton Gardens, a beautiful street of very plush apartment houses. It reminded me a little of Sutton Place: the buildings, the expensive cars at the curb, the starched nanny going by pushing a pram, all reeked of money. I walked around it and maybe I walked along an adjoining street, I'm not sure. Then I turned a corner and found myself on a street I had not been on before and the likes of which I never expect to be on again.

I don't know where I was. I could find no name to the

street, I'm not even sure it was a street. It was a kind of enclosed courtyard, a cul-de-sac behind Clarence House and St. James's Palace. The anonymous white buildings on it might be the backs of the palaces. The white stone glows sumptuous and the street is absolutely still. A footstep is loud and you stand without moving, almost without breathing. There is no reek of money here, only the hallowed hush of privilege. Your mind fills with stories of the fairy-tale splendor of monarchy, the regal pomp of England's kings and queens. And then suddenly you remember Karl Marx in an untroubled grave in Highgate, and Queen Mary welcoming Gandhi as she had welcomed the rajahs before him, as George III had been forced to welcome as Ambassador to the Court of St. James old upstart John Adams. You are awed by the contrasts – by the *fact* of St. James's and Clarence House resting so serenely in Socialist England.

You decide to stop using the word 'anachronism' when a seventeenth-century carriage drives through the gates of Buckingham Palace carrying twentieth-century Russian or African diplomats to be welcomed by a queen. 'Anachronism' implies something long dead, and nothing is dead here. History, as they say, is alive and well and living in London.

Nikki's Barbara phoned this morning; we made a lunch date for Friday. I gave her a couple of questions to ask Nikki over the teletype, she'll bring the answers to lunch with her.

I called the *Reader's Digest* office and the girl there said they're using the fan-mail article in the English edition but it deals only with American fan mail, didn't I have any English fans? Shades of the Colonel, didn't I just. I explained that the article was written and sold before the English fan mail arrived, and she said Would I dreadfully mind writing a page or two about the English fan mail? They go to press in a few days, they would have to have the new pages tomorrow, could I possibly?

I felt like saying, 'Lady, this is the first real vacation I've ever had in my life and I've only got ten days of it left!' But unfortunately it crossed my mind that I wouldn't be having the first real vacation of my life if it weren't for the *Reader's Digest*, so I said it would be a pleasure.

Will now shlep up the street to Deutsch's and borrow a typewriter.

LATER

Wrote three new pages and took them down to the *Digest* office in Berkeley Square and walked home by a lovely new route, straight up the Visitors' Map to the Regent's Park area and then over. Somewhere along the way I came upon a mews with a small sign on the entrance gate addressed to the passing world. The sign orders flatly :

COMMIT NO NUISANCE

The more you stare at that, the more territory it covers. From dirtying the streets to housebreaking to invading Viet Nam, that covers all the territory there is.

There was a letter at the desk for me when I came back :

Can you be here Wednesday at noon *sharp*, for a visit
to two stately homes of England?

In haste —

P.B.

Mary Scott just phoned. She wrote me last spring that
she and her husband are Californians who spend every
spring and summer in London, and she offered to take me on
a walking tour. She told me she's had house guests for a
month, they've just left and she's finally free for that walking tour, she'll pick me up for the tour Thursday morning
and take me home to dinner afterwards.

Tomorrow night I'm having dinner with the English
couple who phoned while I was in Stratford, and the Scotts
are feeding me Thursday, so I may just spring for a hairdresser on the dinner money I'm saving.

Had my hair done at a little shop out Regent's Park way on Paddington Street, and the pretty hairdresser asked Was I from the States, and I said Yes.

'How do you find London?' she asked. 'Do the noise and the crowds bother you?'

The what?

For a big city, London is incredibly quiet. The traffic is worse than at home because the streets here are so narrow; but the cars are very quiet going by in the street and there are no trucks at all, a city ordinance bans them. Even the sirens are quiet. The ambulance sirens go *BlooOOP, blooOOP*, like a walrus weeping under water.

And I haven't seen anything here, not even on a bus, that a New Yorker would describe as a crowd.

MIDNIGHT

Those English fans who invited me to dinner are a charming couple, they live in Kensington in a mews. A mews is an alley built originally for stables and carriage barns, and the fad is to convert the barns and stables into modern homes, everybody wants to live in a converted stable, it's chic.

But stables and carriage barns were built of stone and they don't have windows. And the horses weren't interested in indoor plumbing or electricity. You buy one of these stables and kill yourself turning a horse's stall into a very peculiar kitchen (cramped between two high stone partitions); you wire all the stalls for electricity, you pipe them for water, you get all your kitchen and bathroom equipment and furniture moved into the proper horses' stalls – and when you're all through you still can't chop a hole through a foot-thick stone wall for windows, so you have everything you need but air. The couple I had dinner with live in a charming little stable which, they explained to me cheerfully, is so hot all summer they get out of it as soon after supper as possible. In winter they freeze without heat and suffocate with it.

Across the street from them is Agatha Christie, just as comfortably situated and a lot older.

Demented.

They fed me an elegant salmon steak and drove me through Chiswick – pronounced Chizzick – and we walked along the Strand on the Green. The Strand on the Green is a lovely avenue overlooking the Thames, you can run down the front steps of the houses and jump in the river. The houses were built by Charles II for his mistresses. They are very beautiful and charming, very expensive and sought-after, and the elite who live in them are envied just as much as if the Thames didn't overflow every now and then and flood all their living rooms.

I don't remember what we were talking about, but I described something-or-other in Central Park and my hostess looked at me in horror.

'You mean you actually go into Central Park?' she asked. 'I thought people got killed in there.'

I said I was in it almost every day, and offered to take her and her husband on a guided tour of it if they ever came to New York. And then they told me that last year they spent three days at the Plaza Hotel and never left their hotel room for fear of being killed. They didn't walk down Fifth Avenue. They didn't see the park, even from a hansom cab. They didn't set foot in a single skyscraper. They didn't get on a sight-seeing bus.

They never left their room.

'We were too terrified,' the wife said.

Since I arrived in London, three college boys have been found shot to death as they slept at a camp site; a girl was found stabbed to death in her flat; and there are signs all over town reading LOCK UP LONDON. I asked PB about them, he said they're part of a campaign to get Londoners to lock doors and windows when they go out because of the wave of robberies; three of his friends' flats were robbed in one weekend.

Crime is a hundred times worse in New York. We probably have more murders and muggings there in a week than London will see in a year. Still, for what it's worth, no umpire or fan in Shea Stadium will ever take his eyes off the baseball diamond long enough to make a pass at a girl. And no New York dog will attack three children on the street, killing one of them, which happened here last week.

I mean things are tough all over. Tougher in New York. But not so tough as to justify two Londoners huddling together in a hotel room for a weekend, *declining* the only chance they'll ever have to see the one fabulous city the twentieth century has created.

One of these days I'm going to write a book about living in New York – in a sixteen-story apartment house complete with families, bachelors, career girls, a ninety-year-old Village Idiot and a doorman who can tell you the name and apartment number of every one of the twenty-seven resident dogs. I am so tired of being told what a terrible place New York is to live in by people who don't live there.

PB took me to Syon house, the ancestral home of those miserable Northumberlands who tried to make Jane Grey queen and sided with Mary of Scotland against Elizabeth. The rose gardens there are beyond anything I've seen : acres of roses in a spectacular rainbow of colours. PB told me he spent the weekend with friends in the country who have a double rose garden and didn't offer him so much as a bud to take home. Londoners miss their gardens, he and the other tenants in his building do a little gardening in pots on the roof.

We went from Syon House to Osterly Park, another ancestral home, I forget whose. I'm learning a little about Nash houses and Wren churches; today at Osterly Park it was Adam walls: polished wood panels covered with intricate marquetry. You can examine a single wall for hours and not see all the details in the carving. In a century dominated by watches, cars, planes, schedules, it's hard to imagine an age in which men had the endless time and patience needed for such work.

Driving home, PB told me he worked in Hollywood off and on for years as a consultant on films with English locales. The notion of PB in Hollywood in its heyday, when it was a synonym for everything tasteless and overdone, was grotesque at first, but then I realized he's one of those originals who would be at home in almost any setting; nothing rubs off on him. He's been everywhere and knows everybody, he's very social – there are always a dozen invitations propped up on the mantel – but he seems always a little apart from those around him.

He told me he once spent months hauling an American architect all over England for the Essex House in New York. The Essex House was doing over its cocktail lounge and wanted to re-create an English pub.

'They sent a chap over here to see me and I drove him round the country to see all the best of the old pubs. He went back to New York and drew up the plans and sent them to me. I'll show them to you when we get home.'

We got back to Rutland Gate and he showed me the drawings and they were marvelous: a pub with wood-paneled walls, antiqued wooden tables and benches and a high, old-fashioned wooden bar with kegs above it. The pub looked warm and mellow and the woods burnished in the glow of old-fashioned lamps that swung from the ceiling.

'Is the pub still there?' I asked.

'I think so,' he said.

'I'll go see it when I get home,' I said. 'Did he write and tell you how it looks?'

'Oh, yes' – in that light, noncommital voice – 'the Essex House did the pub in lucite, chrome and black leather.'

He goes to Wales for a week on Saturday. I'll be gone when he gets back.

Mary Scott took me on a walking tour of Knightsbridge and Kensington, we went to Harrods first because I'd never seen it. It's an incredible store, you can buy anything from a diamond necklace to a live tiger, they have a zoo. I thought of Chester, the sheep dog who lives in my building, he came from Harrods.

On the ground floor there's a florist's shop, and if you want to buy a dozen roses you can choose twelve roses individually. You can pick all buds or all open blooms or half and half, and you can buy one of every color in stock. I ran amok rounding up twelve to send to PB to brighten his flat before he leaves for Wales. Didn't know any other way to thank him.

We wandered the mewses and closes and poked into hidden gardens and alleys. Chelsea, Kensington and Knightsbridge all seem to me self-consciously charming, compared with Regent's Park. The Scotts live out that way and I told Mrs. Scott if I were able to take a flat in London it's out Regent's Park way I'd want to live. She said it's not called Regent's Park, it's called Marylebone.

They have a spacious flat on Gloucester Place and she'd made a beautiful salmon mousse for dinner, loaded with cream. Salmon is a great delicacy here; people serve it as a compliment to their guests the way they serve filet mignon or lobster at home.

Got back here about ten and have had the Lounge to myself for an hour but my luck just ran out. A woman just came in looking for somebody to talk to. She says Be sure and see the Temple, locate Middle Temple Lane and you'll see two large white doors leading into the Temple, the Inner Temple and Middle Temple Hall, and the porter will show you the room where Dickens wrote *Great Expectations*. Doesn't seem the time to tell her I found *Great Expectations* very boring, it's the sort of conversation-stopping sequitur you learn is really *non* sequitur.

She says the Knights Templar were buried under the floor

of the church and that's why it's called the Temple. She says the church was destroyed during the war and after the war all the Knights' bones were dug up and they're now in a common grave under the floor of the rebuilt church. It's a good thing I want to see all this, because if I didn't plan to I'd have to keep out of the Lounge, I gather she spends all her evenings in here.

Two women just came in – early thirties, very neat, they may be schoolteachers; they're from Toronto – and it seems the Temple woman sent them somewhere on a day's outing and they are now telling her How Right She Was. Greenwich-by-boat. Maritime Museum.

Temple woman says This will interest me because I'm an American, she says there are Pilgrim artifacts at Greenwich, the Pilgrims took ship from there. Always thought it was Plymouth. Didn't say so. I'm controlling an insane impulse to turn to the three of them and say chattily:

'Did you know that when the Pilgrim Fathers caught a Pilgrim having a love affair with a cow, they not only hanged the Pilgrim, they also hanged the cow?'

One of the teachers wants to know Am I the writer? They've heard such a lot about me at the desk. If they should be able to get a copy of my book tomorrow would I be kind enough to autograph it for them? Soitinly. Told a woman the other night she was passing up a chance to own the only unautographed copy in existence, she just looked at me baffled, nobody understands me.

A man came by at 10 A.M. to interview me for Radio London and I dragged him and his tape recorder over here. I'm not sitting in a dark hotel lobby on a sunny summer morning.

He told me a play was done here last season about Lord Nelson and Lady Hamilton and a script was sent to Buckingham Palace. It came back to the producer's office with a note:

The Duke of Edinburgh thinks you've treated Lady Hamilton very shabbily. The Queen reserves judgment.

Everybody over here has a Philip anecdote for you, they're proud of the fact that he's so unstuffy. It's appealing how people regard the Royal Family as relatives, it's a kind of Cousin-Elizabeth-and-her-husband-and-the-children attitude. So everybody feels free to criticize them, what else are relatives for? Elizabeth, Philip and Prince Charles all very popular. Feelings mixed about Princess Anne; most people I've met are defensive about her. You ask an Englishman:

'What's Princess Anne like?' and the Englishman says:

'Well, you must remember she's still very young, she's new to all this, after all she's only twenty, you can't expect –'

And all you said was: 'What's she like?'

But they're very impressed by her horsemanship, they tell you with great pride: 'She's good enough to ride for England!'

Feelings also mixed (this surprised me) about the Queen Mother. One woman told me:

'Her public image is a masterpiece of press agentry. I once stood next to her at Harrods and caught her eye, and she has the coldest eyes I ever looked into.'

Have to go back to the hotel to meet Nikki's Barbara for lunch. She doesn't like curry but she's being magnanimous and taking me to a curry place near me on Charlotte Street.

There was a thank-you note at the desk when I got back from Russell Square.

The super roses arrived – they are on my desk as I write this and perfume the whole room. How very thoughtful – thank you. I just spoke to Jean Ely, she and Ted arrived at the Connaught last night. I thanked her for introducing us.
Will be back on the 18th. Do be in London still.

In haste –

P.B.

I leave Thursday, the fifteenth.

JULY 6, 1971
TO NIKKI FROM HELENE VIA BARBARA TWO
REQUESTS FIRST ANDY CAPP COMIC BOOKS
OUT OF PRINT COULD YOU THINK OF
SOMETHING MORE CULTURED FOR HER TO
BRING YOU SECOND SHE WOULD LIKE NAMES
OF TWO BEST INDIAN CURRIES SOHO IN THE
NATIVE TONGUE ALIVE AND WELL

TO BARBARA FROM NIKKI MANY THANKS FOR
THE MESSAGE FROM HELENE HER POSTCARD
SOUNDS LIKE SHE IS HAVING A BALL HAVE YOU
MET HER YET

NOT YET BUT AM HAVING LUNCH WITH HER
THIS FRIDAY DO YOU HAVE CURRIES FOR HER

NOT YET WILL CHECK IT OUT WITH MY INDIAN
FRIEND AM JUST BACK FROM VACATION TELL
HER I AM IN LOVE

GOOD FOR YOU BI

JULY 8, 1971
1510 GMT LONDON
TO BARBARA
FROM NIKKI
TWO CURRY NAMES ARE MURGI KARI AND MURG
MASALAM ALSO COULD YOU GIVE HER THE FOL-
LOWING MESSAGE FROM KEN MILLS ALL IS LOST
ROOT FOR DODGERS IN WESTERN DIVISION OR
BETTER STILL TAKE UP CRICKET HAVE FUN
AND THANKS NIKKI END

OKAY NIKKI WILL DO BI

JULY 9, 1971
TO NIKKI NEW YORK
JUST HAD LUNCH WITH HELENE AND SCRIBBLED
OUT THE FOLLOWING MESSAGE FOR YOU
DUCHESS OF BLOOMSBURY STREET SAYS HOW
THE HELL CAN ALL BE LOST ITS ONLY JULY
METS WILL START WINNING WHEN SHE IS HOME
TO ROOT THEM THROUGH DUCHESS SAYS YOU
ARE FORBIDDEN TO ENTER INTO BETROTHAL
WITHOUT HER CONSENT SHE WILL HAVE TO
LOOK HIM OVER FIRST END

I think everybody who works should have Saturday afternoons off, but they have got goofy ways of managing it over here.

Went down to Fortnum & Mason to buy small tokens of esteem for friends back home and by the time I finished it was lunch time. The store has an attractive coffee shop so I went there. There was a long line of people waiting for tables but a few counter seats were empty and I climbed up on a stool and picked up a menu. People were being served on both sides of me and the waitress was rushed. I waited till she'd brought everybody else's tea-and-tart and when she finally turned to me, I said :

'I'll have a—' and she said :

'We're closed, Madam,' and I said :

'You're what?' and she said :

'We're closed.'

And she pointed to a waiter who was carrying a standard to the door. He set the standard down in front of the long line of people waiting for tables and sure enough, the sign on the standard said CLOSED.

At high noon on a Saturday with the store open and jammed with shoppers, the coffee shop closed. Which is what I call having a good strong Union.

Did the Temple this afternoon. It was raining when I came out, I took a bus home. You have to watch it with these buses. A sign on the bus says DO NOT ALIGHT FROM THE COACH UNTIL REQUESTED TO DO SO. Believe me, it's there for your health.

The driver is at one end of the bus with his back to the passengers. Theoretically, the conductor is at the other end, where you get off. But he also has to go through the bus asking new passengers how far they're going and giving them tickets and taking money and making change, and the buses are double decker so half the time he's upstairs.

If he's upstairs when the bus comes to your stop, DO NOT GET OFF THE BUS, just ride past your stop and wait till he comes down. Because if the conductor isn't there to signal the driver when you're safely off, the driver doesn't really stop at your corner, he just slows down there and pauses, and then drives on, on the *assumption* that you're safely off. I'm small and limber, I hopped nimbly off the bus and even so I nearly fell on my face, that bus took off with my left foot on the bottom step.

I just phoned Jean Ely at the Connaught to thank her for asking PB to show me London. She said come to dinner Thursday night, she wants to hear all about it.

I saved my three high spots – the Abbey, the Tower and St. Paul's – for my last week and I'm glad I did. Knowing I'm going to see them has kept me from getting depressed about going home when I'm not ready to go home. Woke in high excitement this morning because Sheila and Nora and I were doing the Abbey this afternoon.

It's full of odd things nobody ever told me about – like a plaque to the memory of Major John André, 'Mourned Even by his Enemies,' it says. 'His Enemies' were us rebels. André was the British spy Benedict Arnold betrayed us to. The Americans caught him and hanged him just as the British had caught and hanged Nathan Hale a little earlier. But you wouldn't believe how many American historians make a much bigger fuss over André's death than they do over Nathan Hale's. Nathan Hale was a poor farm boy, John André was a dashing British aristocrat – see. In class-conscious Philadelphia, where André was stationed, you'd better believe he was 'Mourned by His Enemies.'

It positively outraged me to find Henry Irving buried in Westminster Abbey when Ellen Terry isn't. Henry Irving was one of those legendary actors like Garrick, he was the idol of London in the 1890's. Ellen Terry was his leading lady. I got very fond of her through her correspondence with Shaw and I consider it pure male chauvinism to bury Irving in the Abbey while Ellen's ashes, according to Sheila, are in the little Actors' Church near Covent Garden Market, I'm going there.

Sign of the times: there's a long bench now placed over one grave so all you can see of the inscription is 'Rudyard Ki————.'

We passed the War Office when we came out. It was hot today – eighty-four degrees, very hot for London. Outside the War Office, sitting on a horse in the hot sun, was a guard. He wore a solid brass helmet-and-noseplate, which must have been blazing hot. He was dressed in a heavy wool uniform, long leather gloves and leather knee boots, he had a Persian lamb saddle rug tucked around him and he was clutching a spear which was bending slightly from the heat. Bundled up for the Russian Front, all by himself on a hot Sunday, he was guarding the atomic secrets of the War Office with a bent spear. Him and his fur-covered horse.

Sheila says he's there to please tourists like me, he's the fancy-dress London we come looking for. Maybe so. But far away in Wales I could hear a light voice remarking:

'They haven't missed a night in seven hundred years.'

On the way back to Highgate for dinner we stopped off at Waterlow Park; it's so high above the city the legend on the park sundial informs you:

THIS SUNDIAL IS LEVEL WITH THE
DOME OF ST. PAUL'S CATHEDRAL

and when you look across the hills the dome is level with your eyes.

In the center of the park there's a two-story house with a high balcony, Sheila told me Charles II built it for Nelly Gwyn. Nell bore him a son there and she kept asking Charles to give the baby a title and Charles kept putting it off. So one day, when she saw the King riding toward the house to visit her, Nelly walked out onto the balcony with the baby in her arms and called down to him:

'If you don't give your son a proper title this instant I shall drop him to his death!'

And Charles II cried:

'Madam, don't drop the Duke of—!' and that's how the baby got his title.

LATER

Ena just phoned, they're back. They want me to have dinner with them tomorrow night and then see their flat in Ealing. She and Leo will pick me up here at hoppusseven. Nobody over here says 'six-thirty' or 'seven-thirty,' they say 'hoppussix' and 'hoppusseven.' And 'in' at home is 'trendy' here and 'give it up' is 'pack it in' and 'never mind!' is 'not to worry!'

And when they pronounce it the same they spell it differently. A curb's a kerb, a check's a cheque, a racket's a racquet – and just to confuse you further, jail is spelled 'gaol' and pronounced 'jail.'

And a newsstand's a kiosk, a subway's the tube, a cigar store's a tobacconist's, a drug store's a chemist's, a bus is a coach, a truck is a lorry, buying on time is hire purchase, cash and carry is cash and wrap and as Shaw once observed, we are two countries divided by a common language. I am now going to bed because it's quataposstwelve.

O Frabjous Day!

From now on I remember the *Reader's Digest* in all my prayers. I picked up mail at the desk, there was a letter from the London *Digest* office, I assumed it was page proof on the three new pages. I opened it and inside was a check for FIFTY POUNDS, I thought I would die where I stood.

I hunted up Mr. Otto and asked if I could keep the room an extra ten days, he was shocked at the question, he said, 'Did you think we'd put you out?!' and clucked.

I tore up the street to Deutsch's to tell everybody the news and Carmen said Ann Edwards of the *Sunday Express* wants to interview me Wednesday over lunch.

'And guess where? The River Room of the Savoy! It's the most divine place in London, I'm so happy for you.'

Mr. Tammer couldn't cash the check for me, he said it's made out in such a way only a bank can cash it. Will take it to the bank tomorrow.

I phoned Nora and told her the news and she wants to give a buffet supper for me on Friday to meet all the rare-book dealers, she wanted to do it before but they were all 'on holiday.'

Joyce Grenfell phoned about dinner tomorrow night, she's putting a note in the mail with complete instructions for finding their flat by bus. It impresses me that in London you can mail an in-city letter on Monday and know for certain it will arrive on Tuesday. In New York you can mail a letter on Monday to an address a block away – and maybe it'll get there on Wednesday and very possibly it won't get there till Thursday.

My social life being what it is, I just faced the fact that I can't get along for two more weeks on one dress. God bless my Democratic Club and my brother, am off to Harrods with the gift certificate and the last of the cash reserve, Ena says they're having a close-out sale of summer dresses.

Harrods sale overpriced and mostly midi-skirts they got stuck with. I went up the street to Harvey Nichols and bought a toast-and-white linen on sale and then went back to Harrods and swapped the gift certificate for a sand-colored shoulder bag on sale. Transferred everything to it and threw my old white straw in a Harrods' wastebasket, it's been unraveling for a week.

Took a cab to Johnson's house and lunched at the Cheshire Cheese (money means nothing to me) and stopped at the *Evening Standard* to see Valerie – the girl who interviewed me the day I landed – to tell her the *Standard*'s interviewing me over again. (Now-that-I've-been-here-how-do-I-like-it.) While I was there, the catch on my new shoulder bag broke. Valerie was very shocked; I said, 'That's why it was on sale.' She said, 'Yes, but not *Harrods*!' Nobody ever says 'Bonwit's' in that tone.

She sent me to a little shop off Fleet Street to have it fixed, and while the man repaired it for me I asked if he could point me toward Bloomsbury, I wanted to walk home. He said :

'Go on up to O-burn Street and follow the bus.'

Looked for O-burn Street, looked for Auburn Street and finally stumbled on the street he meant : High Holburn. And that's what they mean by a cockney accent.

Time to go crouch under that sadistic shower and then climb into the new dress for Leo and Ena.

MIDNIGHT

Leo took us to dinner at a plush seafood restaurant. The shellfish looks the same here as at home but tastes very different; the crabmeat and lobster are much richer here but very bland, almost tasteless to an American palate till you get used to it.

They drove me to their flat and I saw Ena's portraits of Hayley Mills and Pamela Brown. Pamela Brown I have a special love for, dating back to an old, old English film called *I Know Where I'm Going* and to a stage performance I saw her give in *The Importance of Being Earnest.*

I know nothing about painting, not even the right thing to say when you like it; but those faces spoke to you. I was bowled over, I told Ena it's indecent to be that talented when you're pretty and blond and look fresh out of school.

Leo announced he was going to make me his special summer drink, for which he is famous, and he trotted off to the kitchen and banged around and came back with three long, tall drinks. I don't drink after dinner and I don't like carbonated drinks so I don't know one long-tall-drink from another. I sipped this one and said:

'It's ginger ale, isn't it? It's very nice.'

'It's gin and tonic,' said Leo, wounded.

'The gin kind of gets lost, doesn't it?' I said, and he loped back to the kitchen for the gin bottle. Ena was doubled up with unkind wifely laughter.

'That's his special drink, he's so proud of it!' she gasped and went off into convulsions. I felt terrible. I told Leo I go through life saying the wrong thing. He put some more gin in my drink and then sat and watched me as I sipped it. When he thought I had enough of it inside me, he said:

'The little thing wants to ask you a favor.'

I looked at Ena and said, 'What's the favor?' but she just smiled nervously. And Leo said:

'She wants to paint you.'

And I said:

'You're crazy.'

I know that painters see planes and angles in faces that look commonplace to the rest of us – and I still cannot understand why anyone should want to paint a plain, ordinary middle-aged face. Which I told Ena. To her, I have an interesting face, 'it changes all the time.' I said I wished it would.

I never felt so trapped. All my life I've avoided being photographed – and here was Ena asking earnestly Would I sit for her? She'd only need a few sittings, 'p'raps three or four?' Anxious little face peering at me wistfully.

I told her I'd do it on two conditions: one, she has to paint me in Russell Square, I'm not sitting indoors in some studio; and two, she has to promise not to make me look at the portrait either in progress or when it's finished.

She agreed to both conditions. She's finishing something this week, we start next week.

Paranoid morning.

Joyce Grenfell's note arrived with instructions for finding her flat tonight but nothing on how to find St. Mary Le-Beau's Church in Cheapside for her dialogue with the minister at noon. I located Cheapside on my map and then decided to get the *Digest* check cashed before I went down there.

I went to the nearest bank and then to another one across the street from it. Both banks were shocked to be asked to cash a *Reader's Digest* check for a total stranger whose identification they declined to look at. Neither would phone the *Digest* or Deutsch's for me, it wasn't bank policy.

I went to a third bank, where a teller passed me on to an officer who conferred with another officer and then came back and said Wouldn't it be better if I just mailed the check to my bank in New York? I explained that I needed the cash here, which shocked him deeply. You do not say 'I need cash' to a banker.

I told him my New York bank was Chemical and asked whether there was a branch in London. He said Yes, reluctantly, but he doubted whether the London branch would cash the check. (He said 'could.') I went down to Chemical — and after asking to see everything but my teeth, they cashed it. Nothing infuriates me like those friendly, folksy bank ads in magazines and on TV. Every bank I ever walked into was about as folksy as a cobra.

By this time I had barely half an hour to get down to Cheapside. I got on a bus and discovered I'd forgotten my map. I told the conductor I wanted to go to St. Mary Le-Beau's, Cheapside, and he let me off down near St. Paul's, pointed to a yonder street and said :

'Walk that way a bit and turn left.'

I walked that way a bit and turned left and walked this way a bit and turned left and turned right and asked six people, all of whom turned out to be tourists. A bus slowed down at a corner, I called to the conductor Could he tell me how to get to St. Mary LeBeau's Church and he called back:

'Sorry, luv, it's m'first day on the job!'

I wished him luck, you might as well, and kept on walking. Found three wrong churches, a Goldsmith's Hall and a lot of interesting alleys but no St. Mary LeBeau's. By this time the dialogue was over anyway and I holed up in a smoky little pub and ate myself pleasant.

MIDNIGHT

Joyce met me at the door and took me on a guided tour of the living-room walls, hung with Grenfell and Langhorne family portraits and photographs. Her mother was one of the Langhorne sisters of Virginia. One sister married Charles Dana Gibson and was the original Gibson Girl, another married Lord Astor and was the famous Lady Astor, MP., and the third married Joyce's father.

Very few theatrical photos on the wall. The one she's proudest of is the Haymarket marquee with her name in lights. The Haymarket has a rule against putting a star's name in lights, it only lights the name of the show. But when Joyce did her one-man show there, she wasn't just the star, she was the show.

She gave me a biography of Florence Nightingale she thinks I'll like. She sets her alarm for six every morning and reads in bed till seven; she said if she hadn't formed that habit, she'd never find time to read anything. As it is, it seems to me she's read everything.

I'm always so ashamed when I discover how well-read other people are and how ignorant I am in comparison. If you saw the long list of famous books and authors I've never read you wouldn't believe it. My problem is that while other people are reading fifty books I'm reading one book fifty times. I only stop when at the bottom of page 20, say, I realize I can recite pages 21 and 22 from memory. Then I put the book away for a few years.

After dinner they drove me around Chelsea and showed

me the house where they were married. Joyce told me they were almost childhood sweethearts.

'I was seventeen and Reggie was just down from Oxford. The first time I played tennis with him I still wore my hair in a braid, I only put it up in the evening.'

They drove down into the old City of London and showed me St. Mary LeBOW's Church, it now turns out you spell it. Only the English could tack 'bow' onto 'le.' Too dark for me to see where I went wrong.

They kept up an amiable running argument about what to show me.

'Oh, not St. Paul's, dear, she'll have seen that.'

'She might like to see it illuminated, RegGEE !'

'She's probably seen it illuminated half a dozen times, why don't you show her Fleet Street?'

I piped up from the back seat that I'd like to see London's slums.

'I'm afraid,' said Joyce gently, 'there aren't any.'

Add that fact to Britain's free medical care and you know all you need to know about the difference between Capitalism and Socialism.

Ann Edwards of the *Sunday Express* took me to lunch at the Savoy and refused to believe I wasn't disappointed in London.

'When I heard you were coming,' she said, 'I wanted to write you and say, "My dear, don't come. You're fifteen years too late." '

For what, Westminster Abbey?

I tried to tell her that if you've dreamed of seeing the Abbey and St. Paul's and the Tower all your life, and one day you find yourself actually there, they can't disappoint you. I told her I was finally going to St. Paul's when I left her and I could guarantee her it wouldn't disappoint me. But she's lived in London all her life, she harks back wistfully to the days when her family owned an upright Rolls Royce, 'which, every time it started, coughed gently, like a discreet footman.'

The Savoy River Room is beautiful and the food marvelous. (I liked Claridge's better but I romanticize Claridge's.) Had crabmeat and lobster thermidor both, couldn't eat my way through either, the portions were enormous, I finished up with strawberries and cream all the same. English cream is addictive – and every time I eat strawberries here I think of the English clergyman who remarked :

'Doubtless God could have made a better berry than the strawberry and doubtless God never did.'

She walked down along the Embankment with me after lunch and pointed me the straightest route to St. Paul's.

It was lovely to walk along the river with John Donne's cathedral looming ahead. Thought about him as I walked, he's the only man I ever heard of who actually *was* a rake reformed by the love of a good woman. He eloped with the daughter of the Lord Lieutenant of the Tower and her outraged papa had them thrown into the Tower for it. John was in one wing, his bride was in another, and he sent her a note, which is how I know he pronounced his name Dunn, not Donn. The note read:

John Donne
Anne Donne
Undone.

He was also a little batty. When Anne died, he had a stone shroud made for himself, and he slept with that shroud in bed with him for twenty years. If you write like an angel you're allowed to be a bit cracked.

I walked up the steps of St. Paul's – finally, finally, after how many years? – and in through the doorway, and stood there looking up at the domed ceiling and down the broad aisles to the altar, and tried to imagine how Donne felt the night King James sent for him. And for at least that moment, I wouldn't have traded the hundreds of books I've read for the handful I know almost by heart. I haven't opened Walton's *Lives* in ten years, at least; and standing there in John Donne's cathedral the whole lovely passage was right there in my head:

When his Majesty was sat down he said after his pleasant manner, 'Dr. Donne, I have invited you to dinner and though you sit not down with me, yet will I carve to you a dish I know you love well. For knowing you love London I do hereby make you Dean of St. Paul's and when I have dined, then do you take your beloved dish home with you to your study, say grace there to yourself and much good may it do you.'

And as Eliza Dolittle would say, I bet I got it right.

There were guides with large tourist parties in tow, each guide giving the standard lecture, some in English, one in French, one in German, the monotone voices jarring against each other. I got as far from them as I could and wandered around by myself. I went down a side aisle looking at all the plaques and busts, walked around the altar and started back up the other side looking at more plaques and busts. Even so, I almost missed it. It was an odd shape, it wasn't a bust and it wasn't a full-length statue, so I stopped and read the inscription. There in front of me, hanging on the wall of St. Paul's Cathedral, was John Donne's shroud.

I touched it.

There's a small chapel just inside the door, with a sign that says : 'St. Dunstan's Chapel. Reserved for Private Meditation.' I went in and gave thanks.

Fifteen years too late indeed.

Ken Ellis of the London *Reader's Digest* came around this morning with his pretty assistant and a photographer, to take my picture. I put up the usual squawk but my heart wasn't in it (I'd be flying over the Atlantic this minute if it weren't for the *Digest*) and I trotted meekly back to 84 Charing Cross Road with them and had my picture taken sitting on the window sill of the bleak, empty upstairs room. Ken scooped up all the peeled and rusting white letters that once spelled Marks & Co. for me. I want to take them home.

(And one September day when I'm doing my fall cleaning I'll come on them and ask myself, 'What do you want these for – so you can weep over them when you're an old lady?' and throw them out.)

They took me to Wheeler's for lunch (the famous seafood restaurant everybody takes you to) and Ken explained to me why everybody over here hates the new money. It has to do with the Englishman's need to be different. The decimal system is much simpler than the old ha'penny-tuppenny-guinea-tenner-tanner system, but the old money was *theirs*; no other country had it and nobody else could understand it. He said they hate entering the Common Market for the same reason. They don't want to be part-of-Europe, they want to be separate, different, set apart. He illustrated this by quoting an old headline which has become a cliché joke over here. During a spell of bad weather when the whole island was enveloped in fog, one English newspaper headline read : FOG ISOLATES CONTINENT.

I'm having dinner with the Elys and Jean just called to warn me that the Connaught is very old-world and still doesn't admit women in pants to the dining room, told her with dignity I have two dresses.

11 P.M.

The Connaught is near Grosvenor Square so I went there first to see the Roosevelt Memorial. Somebody told me that

195

after Roosevelt's death the British government decided to raise money for the Memorial by public subscription and to limit individual contributions to one shilling so that everyone could subscribe. They announced that the subscription would be kept open as long as necessary to raise all the money in one shilling contributions.

The subscription closed in seventy-two hours.

The story moved me a lot more than the Memorial did. It's a statue of FDR standing tall, holding a cane, cape flying. The features are there; the character and personality are entirely absent. And I resent a statue of FDR standing, on legs that were shriveled and useless throughout his White House life. You can't take the measure of Roosevelt if you ignore the fact that his immense achievements were those of a man paralyzed from the waist down. I'd carve him sitting, with the blanket he always spread over his knees to hide the withered legs. Anything else belittles the gallantry and humor in that indomitable face. Since the gallantry and humor are missing from the statue's face I don't suppose it matters. It's nice to know so many Englishmen loved him, anyway.

Jean and Ted Ely still astonish me. They invited me to dinner in New York after they read the book. They live in a very gracious Fifth Avenue apartment, all polished mahogany and old carpets and warm colors, and I thought they were the most beautiful couple I'd ever seen. Both of them are slim and straight, both have thick gray hair, regular features and serenely smooth faces – and when Jean told me casually they were in their mid-seventies I was stupefied. They are as improbably handsome and untouched by time as the parents of the debutante in a 1930's movie.

We talked about PB through dinner. I sent him a note to tell him I'll be here another two weeks, Jean said maybe he'll take the three of us somewhere.

A chauffeured limousine drove me back here; I do not know how anybody expects me to adjust to life on Second Avenue when I get home.

Ena phoned, How's Sunday morning, am I free to Sit? The things I agree to with a little gin in me.

Just got back from Nora's buffet supper – where I arrived an hour and a half late and I was the guest of honor, I mean this evening got off to a horrendous start.

Nora had phoned this morning to say a car would pick me up here at seven-fifteen, so as usual I was dressed and waiting in the lobby at seven. No car came at seven-fifteen, no car came at seven-thirty, and by seven-forty-five I decided Nora's friends must have forgotten to pick me up and I called her. She said she'd ordered a cab for me 'to bring you out in style.' It never came. She told me to go out in the street and hail a cab and come on out.

I went out in the street and hailed a cab and got in. But North London is apparently equivalent to the far end of Brooklyn, and London cab drivers are grimly equivalent to New York cab drivers. I gave the driver Nora's address, and he stared at me mask-like.

'I don't know where that is, Madam,' he said in a flat voice. I innocently explained it was in Highgate. He stared straight in front of him this time and repeated in the same expressionless voice :

'I don't know where that is, Madam.'

I got the message and got out of the cab and waited ten minutes for the next cab to come along and got in. I gave the driver Nora's address, and we went through the same charade. But this driver was so anxious to get rid of me that when I got out of the cab he shot off before I'd gotten both feet on the ground, and I fell and split my leg open. So there I was, blood all over my leg at eight-fifteen of a seven-thirty supper in my honor. I couldn't go back up to the room and clean the wound and put on fresh stockings because that would have made me fifteen minutes later still.

I went back into the lobby and consulted the desk clerk and he said what I needed was a minicab, they take you anywhere. Minicabs are the London equivalent of New York's limousine services (and cost as much). The clerk phoned the minicab service for me and a cab arrived ten minutes later. The driver told me his name was Barry, he's a hospital intern, he drives a minicab nights to earn a little money. He took the hills of North London like he had a death wish for both of us, but never mind, he got us there and gave me a high old time on the way.

He told me he studied at McGill in Canada and spent summers working in Manhattan. The first day he landed in New York he found himself on the traffic island at Broadway and Forty-second Street, he didn't know where he was, he just knew he wanted to go to Times Square. There was a cop directing traffic, and Barry, wanting to ask directions, stepped up behind the cop and tapped him on the shoulder. Whereupon the cop, true to the tradition of courtesy and helpfulness of New York's Finest, turned around and stuck the muzzle of a gun in Barry's stomach.

'I only want to ask directions to Times Square, Officer,' said Barry.

'Izzat right,' said the cop.

'I'm a tourist, I don't know my way about,' Barry explained. 'I'm British.'

'No kiddin',' said the cop without taking his gun out of Barry's stomach. So Barry gave up and said:

'Officer, if you're going to shoot me, please step back so you don't kill the four hundred people behind me.'

The cop let him go then, and Barry crossed the street and asked a passer-by how to get to Times Square. The passer-by studied the problem thoughtfully and then said:

'Walk one block, turn left, walk one block, turn left, walk one block, turn left and you'll be there.'

So Barry walked around the block and that's how he discovered he'd been standing on Times Square all the time. He'd been looking for an English Square – with a park in it. What the passer-by didn't know was that in London you can walk one block, turn left, walk one block, turn left, walk one block, turn left – and be nowhere near where you started from.

He sold Britannicas and fountain pens door-to-door. Most of the housewives slammed the door in his face ('I used to have to call, "Madam, will you please open the door so I can get my tie back?"') so he switched to demonstrating fountain pens at Woolworth's. He discovered the way to beat that system was to get very good at it and be promoted to teacher. 'Teaching other guys how to demonstrate,' he explained, 'you at least got to sit down.'

He dropped me at Nora's and said he'd pick me up at midnight for the return trip.

I could have brained Nora, she hadn't told the guests I'd been ready and waiting since seven-fifteen. One woman turned to me and said politely :

'Do you mind my asking what held you up?' and I was so stunned I couldn't answer her, I just fled upstairs with Sheila and hid out in her room till I got calmed down. I have no poise.

All the rare-book dealers regaled me with stories of the trade. They told me that after the war there were too many books and not enough bookshop space, so all the dealers in London BURIED hundreds of old books in the open bomb craters of London streets. Today the buried books would be worth a fortune if they could be recovered, if the new buildings could be torn down and the rebuilt streets torn up. I had a sudden vision of an atomic war destroying everything in the world, except here and there an old book lying where it fell when it was blasted up out of the depths of London.

Everybody brought me small gifts and I think I made a faux pas with one of them. A very charming woman who deals in autographs gave me a beautifully bound pocket notebook. I needed one, since I'd converted my old one into a calendar, and when the rare-book man from Quaritch's gave he his name and the address of the shop, I wrote them down in the new notebook. From the quality of the silence that followed, I think writing in that notebook was a kind of desecration. I had a horrible feeling the notebook was one of those antique items you're not supposed to use, you're just supposed to look at it. What the hell do I want with a notebook you can't use? I get in trouble this way all the time.

Barry arrived on the dot of twelve and drove me home. He told me to visit his hospital if I get down that way, it's

St. Bartholomew's, he said Go in by the Henry VIII gate and see the chapel, it's beautiful. I wrote his name – Barry Goldhill – in the desecrated notebook and asked him what he's specializing in. He said, 'Gynecology.' I said, 'Too late, honey, I can't do a thing for you.'

Note in the mail from Rutland Gate, he's back.

See you here, Monday, 19th, at 11 *promptly* for sherry
with Charles II and lunch with Charles Dickens.

In haste –

P.B.

I thought I'd better bone up on Dickens first, so after
breakfast I walked out to the Dickens House in Doughty
Street. It's only a few blocks beyond Russell Square, I just
never had enough interest in Dickens to go there before –
which you don't tell to ANYbody over here, it is flat heresy
not to like Dickens. I mean Dickens is the national household god.

Except for PB, not one single Londoner has ever mentioned Shakespeare's pub to me. Nobody mentions the
Pepys landmarks, nobody mentions Wimpole Street – and
nobody knows what you're talking about when you ask
about the house where Shaw courted his 'green-eyed mil-
lionairess.' But every living soul tells you where Mr. Pickwick dined and where the Old Curiosity Shop is and Do see
the house on Doughty Street where *Oliver Twist* was written and This is Camden Town, where Bob Cratchit lived
and The-porter-will-show-you-where-Dickens-wrote-*Great-
Expectations*.

Doughty Street is another of those streets lined with the
gentle, narrow brick houses that still shake me. The Dickens
House is furnished much as it was when he lived in it, and
the room at the back of the house where he worked has a
complete set of Dickens first editions. Walls of every room
are crammed with cases of Dickens memorabilia – letters,
drawings, cartoons, theatre programs with his name in the
cast list. (Never knew he was such a rabid amateur actor.)
All the tourists going through the house, mostly from 'the

U.K.,' knew every character and every incident depicted in every drawing and cartoon. Just incredible.

I had lunch at Tanjar's, the curry place on Charlotte Street, and then walked down to Covent Garden to see Ellen Terry's ashes. The church is called St. Paul's Covent Garden but when you get to the Market there's no church in sight. Wandered around, peering at my map and then at Covent Garden Market. A young man with a brown beard came breezing along, went past me, wheeled, came back and inquired :

'Lost, luv?'

I told him I was looking for the Actors' Church and he said : 'Are you an actress?'

I said No, but I'd been a frustrated playwright in my youth and I loved the Shaw-Terry correspondence and wanted to see Ellen's ashes.

'Isn't that dear of you,' he said. 'Nobody ever comes looking for our church but people in the profession.'

He's an actor. Out of work. He said Just keep going round the Market till you come to an alleyway, cross it and turn the corner and you'll see the church.

I thanked him and wished him luck and he said, 'Luck to you, too, luv!' and went breezing on his way – and looking after him I purely hated myself because I hadn't bothered to ask his name. People oughtn't to breeze into your life and out again in ten seconds, without leaving even a name behind. As Mr. Dickens once pointed out, we're all on our way to the grave together.

I picked my way through the rotting fruits and vegetables lying on the pavement in front of the Market, walked to the corner and came to the alley, a kind of open square used for parking produce trucks and littered with garbage. I crossed the alley and turned the corner and there it was – a small church in a green churchyard, with a garden beyond.

The church was empty. For which I was grateful. I am emotional, and if you're emotional you never know what may suddenly move you to tears. I thought Ellen's ashes might.

There was a pile of mimeographed sheets on a table, and

a sign invites the visitor to take one and sit down and read it so you'll know 'something about where you are.' The church was built by Inigo Jones back in the 1630's. William S. Gilbert was baptized there, Wycherley is buried there, Davy Garrick worshiped there – and Professor Enry Iggins first saw Eliza Dolittle selling her flaaars under the church portico in the rain.

I went along the right-hand wall reading plaques to the memory of long-dead actors and composers. Almost at the end of the wall, near the altar, in a niche behind iron grill-work in a silver urn polished to a pristine gleam, Ellen Terry's ashes. Surprised to find myself smiling at the urn; it's a luminous, cheerful sight.

I crossed the nave and came back up along the left-hand wall and read more plaques clear to the door. Just inside the door as I was leaving I came upon the most recent plaque:

VIVIEN LEIGH   D. 1967

and was suddenly moved to tears.

Sat.

Ena picked me up in a clattery station wagon and drove me to Russell Square and parked at the entrance. The station wagon has sliding doors which I naturally tried to open outward, nearly broke the door and my arm both. Ena was convulsed, she said : 'You're exactly like Leo !' It seems he never gets the hang of anything mechanical either.

I got out and she climbed out after me, all five feet of her, lugging a six-foot easel, a four-foot box of paints, a palette, some magazines and a radio the size of a portable TV set. I wasn't allowed to help : the Subject is not permitted to fetch-and-carry.

We set up deck chairs – lounge chair for me, straight-backed one for her – and I was surprised and relieved to learn that when you Sit you don't have to sit still and hold a pose. Ena told me I could lie back, sit up, stretch, move, smoke, anything as long as I kept facing her. She then went into great detail about how to operate the radio; it turned out she'd brought the radio and magazines for me, to keep me from getting bored. It struck me funny.

'I don't get bored in Russell Square and I don't get bored with you,' I told her. 'Can't we talk while you work?'

'Oh, I'd love that,' she said. 'None of my subjects ever talks to me. They sit in silence hour after hour.'

'With me,' I said, 'that is not likely to be your problem.'

My friend the ticket taker came over to stand behind her and watch her paint. So did two English ladies, an Indian student and a middle-aged Jamaican with a walking stick.

'How's she doing?' I asked them, only wanting to be sociable. But being spoken to directly seemed to embarrass them and they mumbled, 'Very good,' and, 'Very nice,' and melted away. Ena thanked me, she said the gallery made her nervous. So from now on my function is to shoo away what New Yorkers call the Sidewalk Superintendents. In London you shoo them away by talking to them. In New York talking to them would just get you their life stories.

It's fascinating to watch a portrait painter work. There

204

Ena sat, her red-and-white gingham dress flouncing around her, looking completely relaxed, talking, laughing, asking questions as she painted – and all the time, her eyes were darting with incredible speed up to my face, down to the easel, up to the face, down to the easel, up-down up-down up-down, in a motion as quick and sharp and rhythmic as a metronome at high speed. Hour after hour she talked and laughed and painted, and the quick up-and-down darting of the eyes never stopped for an instant. I tried it myself for about twenty seconds and my eye muscles were sore.

She painted till one and then drove me down to Kensington for lunch. We didn't try to talk on the way; the stationwagon clatter was as deafening as a New York subway. English cars are blissfully quiet going by you in the street but very noisy to ride in. American cars exactly the opposite.

She took me to a little Italian place for lunch, down near where she and Leo live, called Panzer's Pasta and Pizza, it's their favorite neighborhood hangout. I had the best martini I've had in London and a chicken-with-garlic-butter they can serve me in heaven.

Ena was shocked that I hadn't been to a single gallery and firmly dragged me to the National Portrait Gallery after lunch – where I amazed myself by going clean out of my mind meeting old friends face-to-face. Charles II looks exactly the dirty-old-man he was, Mary of Scotland looks exactly the witch-on-a-broomstick she was, Elizabeth looks marvelous, the painter caught everything – the bright, sharp eyes and strong nose, the translucent skin and delicate hands, the glittering, cold isolation. Wish I knew why portraits of Mary and Elizabeth always look real and alive, and portraits of Shakespeare, painted in the same era and the same fashion, always look stylized and remote.

I stared at every face so long we never got out of the sixteenth and seventeenth centuries. We're going back next week for the eighteenth and nineteenth, I am now passionately determined to see everybody.

The Colonel phoned, he's driving me into the country for dinner on Wednesday.

Got to Rutland Gate at eleven. That's a lie. I'm always so afraid I won't get there '*promptly*' I always take a cab, I always get there twenty minutes early and walk around the neighborhood till it's late enough to ring his bell. I enjoy it, it's an interesting neighborhood.

He took me to the Old Wine Shades in Martin Lane, Cannon Street, for sherry-at-eleven. It's the only pub in London that survived the Great Fire of 1666. It was built before 1663 and doesn't seem to have changed since. There are ancient wine kegs over the bar, the wooden tables and benches are age-stained, even the menu sounded archaic, I could imagine Sam Pepys ordering the Veal and Sweetmeat Pie.

He took me to the Bank of England, where the doormen and floorwalkers are dressed in red waistcoats and breeches, and bow as they bid you good morning. (Aside from them, it's just one more folksy cobra.)

We had lunch at the George & Vulture where, it quotes on the menu, 'Mr. Pickwick invited about five-and-forty people to dine with him the very first time they came to London.' The restaurant is the headquarters of the Pickwick Club. Dickens cartoons on the walls; steaks and chops done over an open fire in a great stone fireplace.

Around the corner from the George & Vulture is 'the Church of St. Michael Cornhill with St. Peter Le Poer and St. Benet Fink.' I'm putting St. Benet Fink on my favorite Saints list right under the two New Orleans saints.

Back around 1801, when the U.S. bought Louisiana, American firms moved in on the Catholic icon business and began sending crates of church statuary down to New Orleans. The crates were labeled FRAGILE and EXPEDITE. New Orleaners were French, they couldn't read English and they didn't know what the two words meant. They decided the words must be the names of two new saints whose icons were inside the crates. Next thing anybody knew, the most popular saints in New Orleans were St. Fragile and St. Expedite.

St. Fragile lost ground after a while but the last I heard you could still pick up a New Orleans newspaper any day and read in the Personals Column :

> Thanks to St. Expedite for
> special favor granted.

According to the icons, he's an ancient Roman, he wears a toga. Wish I knew as much about St. Benet Fink, PB didn't know who he was.

We walked Lombard Street, PB said the London banking business was founded by Jews from Lombardy in the 1400's. Each money lender hung out an emblem to identify his establishment, and from then on Lombard Street banks all hung out emblems on brass plates. The emblems still swing in the breeze : the Bank of Scotland's emblem is a Cat-and-a-Fiddle, another bank has a Grasshopper, a third has a Rampant Horse. PB didn't know where the symbols came from or what they originally meant, they're hundreds of years old. (So along comes the U.S. and opens a bank on Lombard Street and sees all these cats-and-fiddles and grasshoppers and rampant horses and says, 'Lissen, we oughta hang out something!' and promptly hangs out an American Eagle, we have no national imagination.)

PB is driving Jean, Ted and me into the country to a stately home on Saturday. He upset me by taking me into a jeweler's to approve a lapel pin he's having made for me. It's gold with the red-and-white crest of the City of London.

Will see him Saturday for the last time, they'll have the pin ready then.

I got to Russell Square before Ena, and my friend the ticket taker, after setting up a chair for me, folded his arms behind him, leaned down and inquired conspiratorially :

'Are we anybody we should know?'

Assured him we weren't anybody, and he shook his head reproachfully.

'Painters,' he said, 'do not paint portraits of Just Anyone.'

I told him I was a writer but not famous or important, and he took out a little black book and carefully wrote down my name and Ena's, just as Ena came wobbling round the birdbath with easel, paint box, palette and the mammoth radio she still lugs in case I get bored – though all I ever do with it is make rude remarks about the BBC's taste in music. There's only one classical-music station and whoever runs it is a chamber-music nut, that's all they ever play.

Ena told me I've changed her entire attitude toward portrait painting.

'I never painted anyone out-of-doors before,' she said. 'The atmosphere and feeling are quite different. From now on I shall have to decide with each subject whether he or she's an outdoors or an indoors subject. You were quite right : you're an outdoors subject.'

'We're not out here because I'm an outdoor subject,' I said. 'We're out here because I'm a selfish subject.'

I think she'd love to paint all day long, but no matter what I say, she insists on quitting at one because I have so little time left to see anything.

As we packed up and headed for the station wagon, she looked around Russell Square and said pensively :

'You were right about this place. There's a special quality to it.'

It startled me. I'd never said that. Till she said it, I'm not sure I even knew it.

We had lunch at Panzer's and then went back to the National Portrait Gallery, I saw Jane Austen and Leigh

Hunt and Willie Hazlitt and the eerie Brontë portrait – the faces of the three sisters and in the middle a gray wash where Bramwell's face once was.

The story is that Bramwell painted himself and his sisters, and then wiped out his own image in a fit of self-hate. And of course you can't concentrate on the sisters' faces, the portrait is dominated by that gray wash in the middle. You can't help wondering whether Bramwell knew it would be.

The Colonel outdid himself again. I'd forgotten that when we passed Stoke Poges on the way to Stratford I'd wanted to detour to see Gray's churchyard just because the 'Elegy' was my mother's favorite poem. The Colonel didn't forget; he drove me out to Stoke Poges for dinner, though it's a two-hour drive.

We got there just at twilight. Not a soul around and when we entered the churchyard the bells were tolling the knell of parting day.

Gray's mother is buried there. He wrote the inscription on her monument:

> She had many children of whom only one
> had the misfortune to outlive her.

The church is seven hundred years old, very simple and plain. There were fresh wildflowers in the altar urns. Going down the center aisle you walk on ancient graves of parishioners buried centuries ago beneath the stone floor, their names on the stones obliterated now.

The Colonel strolled the graveyard and let me sit in the church by myself. I wished my mother could know where I was. I felt like the child who calls from a new perch: 'Hey, Ma! Look!'

The Colonel's widowed sister-in-law lives near Stoke Poges. She teaches in London and commutes four hours a day, they're as crazy that way here as they are at home. We drove to her house to pick her up for dinner. She lives in a beautiful country suburb that could be anywhere in Connecticut – as Nora's house and suburb might be anywhere in Queens. It's amazing how alike and anonymous all suburbs are, as undistinguishable from one another as highways. Maybe that's why I love cities. There's not a row of houses in London that could possibly be mistaken for New York. There isn't a square block in Manhattan that will ever for a moment remind you of London.

We had dinner at a beautiful pub called The Jolly Farmer. 'Pub' is a very elastic term; it can mean a corner bar, a bar-and-grill, a cocktail lounge or an expensive restaurant. The Jolly Farmer is a typical Connecticut country restaurant: excellent, expensive and relentlessly charming. I had shrimp curry, and when I told the manager it was better than the curry I make, he brought me a jar of his own curry paste to take home to New York.

'Tell me,' the Colonel's sister-in-law said to me over coffee, 'why are all Americans so fond of Gray's "Elegy"?'

Never knew they were, frankly. Except for my mother I never heard any American mention it. But the Colonel's sister-in-law meets a much larger cross section of American tourists at Stoke Poges than I'll ever meet in Manhattan, and they've all come there because of Gray's 'Elegy,' so I took her word for it. And because I didn't have the moral backbone to say, 'I don't know,' I explained the whole thing to her – off the top of my head.

'We are a nation of immigrants,' I said. 'All our forebears were the poor and despised masses of Europe and Africa. We went to school and studied English poetry, and the poets we read all celebrated the aristocracy: kings and queens and Sidney's-sister-Pembroke's-mother and the spires of Oxford and the playing fields of Eton. Except Gray. Gray celebrated the mute inglorious nobodies. And since all Americans are descended from mute inglorious nobodies, I suppose he strikes a chord with us.'

I hope I was right because she and the Colonel believed it. I even believed it myself. Got so carried away by my own eloquence that when we were driving home I began to wonder whether in explaining the American affection for Gray, I'd stumbled on a clue to the English passion for Dickens. They may admire Shakespeare more but it's Dickens they love. Maybe the average Englishman, being neither king nor peasant, identifies less with the kings and peasants of Shakespeare than with the lower and middle-class upward-mobility types in Dickens. Even PB shares the national mania for Dickens – but he told me that one of his great-grandfathers was a fishmonger, and that when he was at Eton he was taunted by the other boys because his mother was 'a Colonial,' born in Australia.

The Colonel is giving a farewell party for me on Sunday night. He'll be at the airport Monday when I leave.

I'm getting so guilty about forcing Ena to paint me out-of-doors in London's well-publicized climate. We were rained out this morning for the second time. Yesterday when we were rained out she drove me to the Tower but there were long lines waiting to get in and I still can't stand on line very long. Today we started for the Tower again, but halfway there the weather cleared suddenly and I made her drive back to Russell Square. We'll do the Tower Sunday, I like having it the last London sight I'll see.

My friend the ticket taker is now entirely carried away by the project. He told Ena solemnly :

'That portrait will be worth hoff-a-million one day.' I told her if it is I get half.

Leo drove up and found us there at six. I could see Ena grinding her teeth, she'd wanted to paint as long as the light lasted. She'd told him we'd be in Russell Square and he should pick us up for dinner, but she counted on his not finding it till seven; like me, he has no sense of direction. He found Russell Square with no trouble at all and it infuriated her. And dear, obtuse Leo, who worships her and didn't know he'd committed a faux pas, went and committed a worse one : he stood behind her with his hands locked behind his back and gazed profoundly down at the portrait (Ena hates a gallery even if the gallery's Leo) and announced to me that it was 'going to be beautiful.' That ended the sitting and we drove down to Panzer's, Ena and I in the station wagon, Leo following in the car. He'd wanted to take me somewhere very grand for our farewell dinner but I told him I'd rather have it at Panzer's.

We were finishing our drinks and were trying to find a day for me to drive down to Chartwell, Churchill's old home, which friends of theirs have bought, when I heard someone say :

'Hello, Helene.'

I looked up and saw coming toward us a woman I've known casually for years. She runs a successful shop in New

York and she's very high-fashion. She's always perfectly friendly and pleasant when we meet but she's never considered me worth more than a passing hello.

I said Well-for-Heaven's-sake-Dorothy, and introduced her to Leo and Ena. Leo invited her to join us for dinner, which she did. She explained she's here on a quick buying trip and she'd just landed. Leo, who has the world's most beautiful manners, ordered dinner for her and then engaged her in conversation so Ena and I could work on the Chartwell problem.

The problem was that since I'm leaving on Monday morning I haven't a free day to go down there with them.

'Tomorrow,' I told Ena, 'Sheila Doel is driving me to Hatfield, it's the only palace I've ever wanted to see; and then we drive back to Highgate for my last dinner with Nora. Saturday is my last day with Pat Buckley, he's taking me somewhere in the country.'

'I want the Manns to meet you,' said Leo. 'If they can have us on Sunday, can you drive down with us then?' And he explained to Dorothy that Christopher Mann and his wife, Eileen Joyce, had bought Chartwell.

'Sunday's the only day we have left for a sitting,' I said. 'I think Ena's counting on it.'

'You need another sitting?' Leo asked, and Ena nodded, and he explained to Dorothy about the portrait painting.

'I don't see why you have to go home on Monday,' said Ena, and sighed. And I sighed. And Leo sighed. And then he turned to Dorothy and asked how long she'd known me. She said vaguely: 'I don't know. Eight or ten years.'

'Tell me,' said Leo in his vibrant English baritone, 'we've only known her a few weeks. Why is it so difficult for us to part with her?'

I turned to Dorothy, ready to say something joking, but I never said it. She was literally open-mouthed, gawking at Leo. She mumbled something and then turned her gaze on me, still open-mouthed, still with that incredulous look on her face. Looking at her, I saw my own inward reaction to being a five-week Duchess mirrored in Dorothy's face.

We left Panzer's and Dorothy thanked Leo for dinner and

declined a lift to her hotel, she said it was just up the street. Then she turned to me and, struggling to make it sound light and teasing instead of plainly baffled, said:

'I don't suppose there's any use asking you to fit *me* into your busy schedule?'

I wanted to say:

'Never mind, Dorothy. Next week the ball will be over and Cinderella will be back at the pots and pans and type-writer in an old pair of jeans and a hand-me-down T-shirt, same as always.'

I just grinned and said I'd see her in New York.

God bless Sheila, Hatfield House was the crowning touch. It's not the oldest palace or the most beautiful, it's just Elizabeth's. She grew up there. One wing of her palace is still standing, we saw her dining rooms – and more of her kitchens than she ever saw of them.

We sat on a stone bench in the garden. It was quiet and deserted and four hundred years dropped away, you could imagine yourself there in the garden with her when the gentlemen of the Council rode up and dismounted and knelt to tell her she was Queen of England.

We drove back to Highgate for dinner and Nora gave me some photographs of Marks & Co. to take home, and one of Frank. She told me how furious she used to be when he brought one of my letters home to read to the family.

'I'd say to him, "What kind of husband are you, to bring another woman's letters home!"'

'If he hadn't brought them home,' I said, 'you'd have had cause to worry.'

She looked at me and nodded.

'That's just what Frank used to say,' she said.

Her garden almost done; she gave me the last of the roses to bring home.

With PB and the Elys to Losely House, an Elizabethan mansion. Elizabeth herself was once a house guest there. And wrote her host a long list of complaints and criticisms when she got home.

The three of them are having dinner tomorrow night at a pub Sam Pepys dined at, they wanted me to come along. I said I'd try to make it before the Colonel's party, I knew perfectly well I couldn't but I'm a coward, I didn't know how to say goodbye-and-thank-you to PB. Will call him tomorrow and say goodbye on the phone.

After we dropped the Elys at the Connaught, he took me to the jeweler's to get my lapel pin. It's a gold crossbar with the red-and-white London seal and the city's motto in gold :

DOMINE DIRICE NOS

Trust He will go on directing them.

Did most of my packing last night so Ena could get an early start in Russell Square this morning, and she painted till noon, when we were rained out again.

She drove me through Regent's Park for a last look at the Nash Crescent and all the lovely streets, and then on down to Panzer's for a farewell lunch before we headed for the Tower.

We drove to the Tower and found people standing on line four abreast, waiting to get in. The line stretched for a city block along the Tower gates, and it wasn't moving. I knew then I would never see the inside of the Tower of London. I could have gone so many times. I let it go too long.

'Next summer,' said Ena brightly, 'we'll make a list of all the places you didn't see and we'll do the Tower first off !'

She's going to drive me to the airport in the morning.

LATER

The Colonel has a comfortable flat in Chelsea and his friends are all pleasant and easy to be with : two men, several attractive widows and a shy young couple from Switzerland. I don't remember any of their names or what we talked about, I couldn't concentrate. The party broke up early since I leave for the airport at 10 A.M. Nora was there. She drove me home and we said goodbye and promised to write.

I'm writing this in bed. With the packed suitcase standing open on the floor, the dresser top bare and the drapes drawn against the rain, the room looks exactly as it did the night I came.

Had the suitcase brought down after breakfast and paid the bill. Phoned PB to say goodbye but no answer.

Went up the street to Deutsch's and autographed twenty copies of the book for Australian booksellers due here tomorrow for a convention. Don't know their names and *still* couldn't bring myself just to write my name and let it go at that, it seems unfriendly. Wrote 'To an unknown booklover' in every copy, sometimes I think I'm crazy.

Said goodbye to Carmen and Mr. Tammer and all the other people at Deutsch, except André, who hadn't come in yet. Then went over and said goodbye to Russell Square. My friend the ticket taker hadn't come on duty yet; I was there by myself.

Came back to the hotel and tried PB again but still no answer. Decided to write him the minute I get home but would have done that anyway. When I came out of the phone booth Mr. Otto bowed and said solemnly:

'Madam's Jag-U-Ar awaits.'

And there was Ena in a borrowed Jag, she said Leo had the car and she wasn't going to drive me to the airport in a station wagon too noisy to talk in.

She gave me a ring set with two small pearls because she once heard me say I like pearls.

The Colonel met us at Heathrow. He had my suitcase taken care of and then led us grandly into the VIP Lounge for sherry. Over sherry, he announced that after my plane left he was going to take Ena on a VIP tour of the airport buildings.

He and Ena walked me to the plane. The Colonel handed me over to a stewardess and told her to take good care of me, and he and Ena kissed me goodbye. I had a seat by the window and I slid into it and peered out, looking for them. Just as I saw them and lifted my hand to wave, they turned away and vanished in the crowd.

The plane lifted – and suddenly it was as if everything had vanished: Bloomsbury and Regent's Park and Russell

Square and Rutland Gate. None of it had happened, none of it was real. Even the people weren't real. It was all imagined, they were all phantoms.

I sit here on the plane trying to see faces, trying to hold onto London, but the mind intrudes with thoughts of home : the mail piled up waiting for me, the people waiting, the work waiting.

Bits of Prospero run in my head :

> Our revels now are ended. These our actors
> . . . were all spirits and
> Are melted into air, into thin air . . .
> The cloud-capped towers, the gorgeous palaces,
> The solemn temples . . . dissolve
> And, like this insubstantial pageant faded,
> Leave not a rack behind. We are such stuff
> As dreams are made on. . . .

Rest in peace, Mary Bailey.